# Christians and the Art of Caring

Books published by The Westminster Press

By William V. Arnold and Margaret Anne Fohl
*Christians and the Art of Caring*

By William V. Arnold
*Introduction to Pastoral Care*
*The Power of Your Perceptions*
(Potentials: Guides for Productive Living)
*When Your Parents Divorce* (Christian Care Books)

By William V. Arnold,
Dixie McKie Baird, Joan Trigg Langan,
and Elizabeth Blakemore Vaughan
*Divorce: Prevention or Survival*

# Christians and the Art of Caring

William V. Arnold
and Margaret Anne Fohl

The Westminster Press
Philadelphia

Book design by Gene Harris

First edition

Published by The Westminster Press®
Philadelphia, Pennsylvania

PRINTED IN THE UNITED STATES OF AMERICA

9  8  7  6  5  4  3  2  1


Library of Congress Cataloging-in-Publication Data

Arnold, William V., 1941–
    Christians and the art of caring.

    Bibliography: p.
    1. Caring—Religious aspects—Christianity.
I. Fohl, Margaret Anne.  II. Title.
BV4647.S9A76   1988    241'.4    87–29394
ISBN 0–664–24073–9 (pbk.)

# Contents

# 1

# A Case for Caring

Sitting on the shelves of every bookstore are multiple books on care, counseling, and other assorted ways of helping people. Right? So why another one?

Well, to start with, we believe that caring is a unique form of helping that finds special expression in the church. This caring is offered by both pastors and members of the congregation. Support groups for people in grief, persons recovering from divorce, parents of dying children, and visitation programs for elderly members are only a few of the special ways in which churches seek to express God's love.

Second, many churches and other caring groups are interested in understanding and implementing the gifts of caring. They know that these gifts are not confined to the ordained clergy. Rather, they belong to all of us who seek to be faithful. Caring is shared by the entire people of God. We are all called to care as a part of our response to the caring we have received through Jesus Christ.

Distinctions do exist between the care offered by trained clergy and that shared by members of a congregation. These distinctions exist in the form of expectations and in degree of training. Ministers are *expected* to respond to parishioners in need and even to take the initiative in reaching out to persons in distress. Congregational members, on the other hand, are not expected to exercise pastoral care unless the church develops a tradition of shared ministry.

Seminarians learn pastoral care skills that enable them to diagnose and intervene in difficult situations. Congregational members do not ordinarily have such professional training. Over time, however, many congregations have benefited by learning skills from their pastor in order to provide a more effective pastoral ministry.

## The Uniqueness of Christian Caring

Caring is a joint effort. But caring is not just something that we *do;* to make that assumption is to think that the caring, in the final analysis, depends on *us.* We do not carry it out by ourselves. Rather, we carry it out with a sense of being accompanied not only by other members of the community of faith but by Christ as well. When we go to visit a hospital patient, it is comforting to know that Christ is with us.

As Christians we believe that we are called to be followers of Christ. That can be a little threatening to think about. The early church formulated creeds affirming the belief that Christ was both fully human and fully divine. We cannot make the same affirmation about ourselves. That is why we would say we are imitators and not substitutes. We are indeed fully human. We are also created in the image of God. The identity we share in that image enables us to be vehicles through which the grace of God can be communicated to others.

Christian caring is a form of helping that consciously calls on our human gifts and God's love. In our humanness we can understand and identify with the pain that a brother or a sister experiences. The problem is, we may identify so much that we lose perspective. We may treat other people as if they were ourselves. Once we do that, we have lost the ability truly to care for *them.*

When we also acknowledge, and even invoke, God's activity in this arena for caring, a person is not receiving help from us alone. We affirm that God is present and that, by God's grace, we can free ourselves of much of the personal baggage that interferes with our helping. When this happens, God's caring is reflected through us, accompanied by the unique gifts that we possess. The old phrase, "Let go and let God," may well be helpful to us here, as long as we don't assume that we don't matter at all. The beauty of Christian caring lies in the cooperation between God's healing power and our own unique way of conveying it.

One of the things we will stress throughout this book is the importance of a close personal relationship with God. This relationship is essential for genuine pastoral caring. It is this combination of our own gifts and our relationship to God that enables us to remain who we are as individuals and allow God's love to flow through us. This is what makes caring within the context of the church unique when compared to other forms of caring. It is not just human work. It is also God's work.

We are aware that many people share our belief in the importance of caring but are uncomfortable *doing* that sort of thing. Their image is one of sitting with people during very emotional times but not knowing the right thing to say (or what not to say!). This discomfort itself may be a sign that you take caring seriously. It *matters* to you that you say and do the right thing. So how can you become more confident and comfortable in communicating your care and concern for others? The fact that you are reading this book indicates that you are interested in caring, either for yourself or for teaching others. What, then, makes *you* uniquely suited for this form of caring?

One factor is your interest. You've probably always been interested in caring for people in some way. You may have been successful in reaching out to people, or you may have been frustrated in those attempts. But the interest is there. You *want* to care. What are some of the ways in which that caring can be expressed effectively? To start, let's explore a fairly typical situation in which people seek to care.

## A Case Study

Mary is the person in the office who is always helpful. She'll watch a colleague's desk and answer the telephone when the person is on break. She's the one who plans the birthday surprise for the boss. And she's always available to listen when someone has a bad day. Many people have described her as an amazing person. She is always helping and never seems to have any needs of her own. In fact, no one can remember Mary ever asking for help. No one knew, for example, that in addition to all the help she provided at work, she was also caring for her terminally ill mother. Last fall, Mary's mother died. She received the news at work on Friday, and word spread quickly through the office.

Joe is Mary's boss. Everyone likes and respects him, because he is both competent and fair in his managerial position. When Joe heard about Mary's mother, he wanted Mary to know that he was sorry and that he cared for her. She was a valuable person, not just an employee. Joe agonized over what to do and say to Mary to show he cared. He rehearsed things to say and even spent thirty minutes trying to pick out just the right sympathy card. He planned to have her come to his office so he could talk privately with her, but he wound up stopping by her desk, touching her on the shoulder, and fumbling with words to express how he felt. He went home frustrated and disappointed with himself for not being able to communicate his feelings and decided not to try again. Caring seemed like so much work, and it consumed so much time.

Joe is a good example of one who genuinely cares, but he simply doesn't know how to express it. What a shame that so much time and energy in caring was never fully expressed to the person for whom it was intended! The frustration leads him to back off rather than risk hurting the other person or being embarrassed.

Dorothy is the veteran secretary in the office. When she heard the news, she immediately called the florist and ordered the usual basket of flowers. One of her co-workers suggested stopping by to see Mary over the weekend, but Dorothy's reply was, "Oh, no. That won't be necessary. She has a minister and a church that take care of that sort of thing."

Dorothy is also a person who truly cares for other people. Her caring centers on the rituals that she has been taught in growing up. She responds on the basis of what is expected, fulfills that duty, and expects others to fulfill theirs. As long as the ritual of caring is accomplished, no further action is needed. Dorothy is a good example of someone who places strong emphasis on order. If things are structured, they will go well. Order and ritual take precedence over spontaneity and searching for more unique responses in various situations.

Frank also cares about Mary, and it was painful for him to hear about her mother's death. He lost his father three months ago and is just now beginning to feel in control of his emotions. He felt that speaking with Mary might cause him to break down again. Besides, when his father died, there were times when Frank wanted to be by himself. Many well-meaning visitors were not aware of his needs and stayed too long. Based on that experience, he concluded that Mary would appreciate being left alone. His own preference for grieving in private hindered his ability to communicate to Mary the depth of his caring.

Frank, like many males in our culture, feels that

any public expression of intense feeling is "bad." He fails to see the healing that can come to himself and others through sharing grief. Frank, then, is a good example of one who places a premium on privacy and control. People are perceived to be better off if they are not seen in their most vulnerable moments.

Roger is the most recent addition to the office staff. He came immediately after graduating from college, where he majored in psychology. His primary interest focused on interpersonal relationships, and so he spent a great deal of time learning communication skills. When he learned of the death of Mary's mother, he eagerly sought an opportunity to put his skills into practice. As Mary was leaving the office, he rushed up to her, and the following conversation took place:

ROGER: Gee, Mary, I'm glad I caught you. I just heard about your mother's death. I'm very sorry.
MARY: Thank you, Roger. It has really been hard.
ROGER: Sounds like it's really been hard for you.
MARY: Yes.
ROGER: You mean it really was tough.
MARY: Yes, that's what I just said.
ROGER: Well, yes, that's what I heard you say, that it's been hard for you, and I really do want to understand.

There was a period of awkward silence. Then Roger walked away, wondering why after all his training, he didn't feel helpful. Mary was left quite puzzled herself about what had just taken place.

Roger is a person who understands caring in a mechanical way. Having learned certain stylized techniques for helping people, he has difficulty using those learned skills to communicate genuine compassion.

Ruth, a friend of Mary's, heard the news and immediately called their minister. Then she called

Mary to ask how she was. Mary began to tell her about the pain and distress she had felt during the last days of her mother's illness. Ruth interrupted with, "Oh, I know just what it was like. I had to take care of my sister up to the very end when she was ill. You know, she had this strange disease that the doctors couldn't diagnose, and I was the only person who would really take care of her." She went on for some time before Mary thanked her for calling and hung up.

Ruth could identify with much of what Mary had gone through. However, she was so busy telling her own story that she missed the opportunity to listen to Mary's pain.

Mary's minister, Charles, received the message from Ruth late on Friday afternoon and called Mary as he was leaving town. He had already telephoned the funeral home and found that initial arrangements had been made. The church's bus was full of high school students ready to leave for their annual retreat. Charles regretted that he couldn't visit Mary just then, but he assured her that he would call on Sunday evening as soon as the group returned. After talking with her, he tried to reach one of the church officers to suggest a visit to Mary, but when no one answered, he gave up and climbed aboard the departing bus.

Charles is a good example of someone who assumes too much responsibility. By allowing, even encouraging, the church to assume that he is the person primarily responsible for care, he contributes to a less effective system for rendering genuine caring.

Six people were very concerned for Mary. They each were trying to provide help in their own way.

But Mary spent the weekend grieving alone.

**For Your Reflection**

The men and women in this scenario illustrate the strengths and weaknesses of different kinds of caring. We will use each of them as a focus in the following chapter. You are encouraged to be more than a detached reader. Think about yourself in relation to each of these persons, including Mary. Take some time to remember incidents of hurt in your own life.

1. What was helpful to you?
2. What seemed to get in the way?
3. What were special times in your life when you wanted and received (or didn't receive) care?
4. What can you learn from this about ways you can be more sensitive in your caring?

*Gracious God, thank you for the love you have given me that I can share with others. Remind me of the special gifts that are mine by your grace and enable me to use them to communicate your love to others. Through Jesus Christ, I pray. Amen.*

# 2

# Developing Your Skills of Evaluation

We want to broaden your understanding of caring and introduce skills that will enable you to care more effectively. We are inviting you to develop an ability to be more observant of both your own needs and the needs of people around you.

This is a basic theological commitment. Think of it in terms of your call to be a Christian. Part of that call involves your commitment to be a part of the priesthood of all believers. The priestly part of you is that part which seeks to help those in need. But another part of you is the finite, limited creature who simply can't do everything alone. This means that all of us are always in need of help in some form, even in those rare moments when we feel most in charge of ourselves and the situation.

We are also very gifted creatures, with the capacity to create and grow in our own lives. Further, we are able to extend help to others in their moments of need. This book is designed to help you identify your own limits and needs in caring situations. We also want to help you recognize the particular gifts that enable you to care for others. This awareness will strengthen your development of effective caring skills as you seek to be more of the human being that God has called you to be.

Mary, Joe, Dorothy, Frank, Roger, Ruth, and Charles care very deeply about other people. They each have particular gifts and particular limits in their expression of care. Through examining their strengths and weaknesses, we hope to help you develop your skills of observation and analysis as well as identify ways we can all grow in the task of caring for each other.

As we examine each of these caregivers, we invite you to join us in assessing their strengths and weaknesses. A model for this process is presented as we look at Mary and Joe. Then, as the other characters are reintroduced, opportunity is provided for your own analysis. We want you to develop this practice of regularly evaluating yourself and others in caring situations. The idea is not to turn you into a judge as much as to get you to view yourself as a perpetual student in the art of caring. Your own perceptions may be different from ours. The important thing is for you to become aware of the multiple dimensions in caring.

### Mary: A Person Who Cares Too Much (page 10)

Mary, in many ways, is a model for caring. When we think of a "good Christian person," the image of a Mary comes to mind. She exerts great energy reaching out to people to care for them, and she is genuinely helpful. Furthermore, people *know* that she is dependable. Her caring is real, her abilities are multiple, and in many ways she *is* a model. We can summarize Mary's strengths:

1. Genuine love and care
2. ·Ability to express that care
3. Willingness to live out that ability
4. Physical and emotional capacity to give

While we applaud these characteristics and commend them as strengths, there is a down side. Mary has more to learn about caring. It really is possible to care too much! In fact, Mary can be characterized as a woman who cares too much. For six years she took care of her invalid mother and for the last three months watched her slowly die of cancer. Throughout this whole ordeal, Mary never asked for any help, although she knew about the local hospice program and had friends at church and generous neighbors. But Mary felt she had to do it all herself. She was unable or unwilling to share her physical and emotional burdens, and therefore she failed to give others the opportunity to be caring to her mother or, for that matter, to her. At the same time, she not only continued working full time at the office but even managed to take care of everyone's needs there, never telling them of her responsibilities at home. The final result was that she created a unique form of isolation that made her burdens seem even more overwhelming.

Perhaps the greatest loss lies in the fact that the image of being the "ultimate caregiver" makes it difficult for a person to admit his or her *own* need for care. Part of caring involves our admitting our limits and allowing *ourselves* to be cared for. Learning to care *for* others necessitates accepting caring *from* others. When we "care too much," we deplete our own physical and emotional energies and rob others of the opportunity to express care to us as well. To summarize Mary's weaknesses:

1. Failure to acknowledge limits
2. Overextension of self
3. Inability or unwillingness to acknowledge her own needs
4. Missed opportunities for *sharing* in caring

### Joe: The Perfect Fit (pages 10–11)

Joe is an excellent manager. He has learned the importance of cultivating personal as well as professional relationships with his employees. When a new task is to be assigned to a worker, Joe is meticulous in writing out a detailed job description. Clarity and fairness are paramount. Personal conversation, inquiry concerning the person's feelings about the task, and follow-up to assure that things move smoothly—all are characteristic of Joe's attention to "his people." He is unusually attentive to fitting the right job to the right person. Not only has this worked well from a business standpoint but his employees respect him. There is a remarkable level of motivation, accompanied by ability, to weave the professional and the personal into the same tapestry of working with his employees. We can summarize Joe's strengths as:

1. A genuine "feel" for people
2. His working hard to "do the right thing"

At the same time, Joe's perfectionism gets in his way. The very skill for which he is noted has a flip side. He worries so much about getting the "perfect fit" that a sort of paralysis sets in. Anxiety about being right blocks his ability to carry through with his caring in intense situations. Without that perfect fit, he gives up, and so Mary never benefited from his caring. Another consequence is that his frustration leads him to "beat up on himself." Ironically, Joe finds it difficult to extend to himself the same care he wants to extend to everyone else. He denies, by his actions, the reality of grace in his own life. Thus Joe's weaknesses are:

1. Assumption that there is only one right response
2. Concern about being embarrassed
3. Unrealistic expectations for himself as a caregiver

## Time Out

Maybe we should stop here and clarify what we are doing with Mary, Joe, and the participants in this case study who are yet to be evaluated. Our objective is not to pick on them. We acknowledge our own limitations, as well as theirs, as we jointly share in caring. Our aim is to cultivate a willingness to look for strengths and weaknesses in order to enrich the caring capacities that lie within each of us. Join us in looking for opportunities to grow in our caring. Mary and Joe both have very real strengths that we have identified, and you may see even more. They each have room for growth as well.

In Mary's case, we would encourage her to continue to express the caring that she does so well. At the same time, we hope she will recognize and be able to take advantage of all the help that is available to her. Learning to receive care protects us from isolating ourselves, relieves us when the burden of caring seems heavy, and renews our perception of the *joint* responsibility that we share in caring for each other.

Our approach with Joe would be to commend him for his depth of caring. In his capacity as boss, it is unlikely that he hears such gratitude very often. People may assume, because he is so good at his job, that he doesn't need affirmation. But we all need praise, especially folks like Joe who are harsh in judging their own performance. Joe needs to hear a word of grace. He needs to know that his caring has value even when it isn't perfect. In fact, Joe made a simple but very important gesture that the others did not. He reached out and touched Mary. (This basic but very powerful means of human communication will be explored in chapter 4.)

Our aim in this discussion is twofold: to identify strengths and weaknesses and to use this analysis as a basis for growth. We aren't interested so much in

grading performance as we are in increasing awareness and encouraging growth.

Now it is your turn to join in evaluating the characteristics of the remaining participants in this case
study. Using the same pattern carried out with Mary
and Joe, list some of the strengths and weaknesses
that you see in each of these men and women. Please
remember that we don't have all the right answers.
We do have our own perceptions, and we hope they
serve as catalysts for your thinking.

### Dorothy (page 11)

What descriptive title fits Dorothy's mode of caring? Stop and take a moment to list the strengths and
weaknesses that you see in Dorothy's style of caring.

Following our pattern of labeling each caregiver,
we have named Dorothy the Rector of the Rituals.
That is a tongue-in-cheek way of emphasizing the
high level of importance that she, like Joe, places on
doing the right thing. If you had a mother who stayed
on your back to write your thank-you notes, you
know what she is like! We see Dorothy's *strengths* as
(1) her genuine desire to do the right thing, (2) her
knowledge of the traditional ways of caring, and (3)
her willingness to take action on the basis of what she
knows.

Her *weaknesses* include (1) the somewhat mechanical nature of her caring, (2) her being stuck in
the traditional modes of caring, (3) her assumption
that others can always be depended upon to do
their job in caring, and (4) her apparent preference
for dealing with the circumstances rather than
with the person.

Dorothy is a valuable member in any community.
While many of us are working hard to be unique, she
is the torchbearer for custom and etiquette. These
traditions communicate value and caring to people

in need and should not be ignored or forgotten. It does seem true that in times of crisis many people become paralyzed. They get so caught up in the feelings of the moment that no action is taken. The Dorothys of the world call the florist while the rest of us huddle and talk about "how awful" it is.

On the other hand, Dorothy's care turns out to be somewhat mechanical. She responds automatically and thus misses the importance of the personal touch that makes caring more genuine. This is what we mean when we say that she deals more with the situation than with the person. When she hears of a birthday, she orders a cake; when she hears of a death, she orders flowers. At this point *her* caring has been done "just right," and she assumes that others will follow through with *their* caring. Surely, she thinks, the minister will provide pastoral care to Mary, because that is the right thing for *him* to do. But in this case, as is too often true, those assumptions were not valid; Dorothy was too trusting. Circumstances often interfere with the right things being done automatically.

Dorothy's form of caring illustrates two essential ingredients to remember in providing care. First, she shows us that rituals are necessary to assure consistency and continuity in caring. For example, the funeral itself is a traditional ritual of caring in our society. It assures the survivors that the community acknowledges their loss, assures them of God's comfort, and encourages them to grieve. However, when the funeral is over, the ritual has been performed, and there is no assurance of further care. (The importance of care after the funeral will be discussed in chapter 5.)

Second, Dorothy was limited in expressing the personal dimension in caring. Flowers and a funeral, important as they are, are not enough. Unique characteristics and needs may be overlooked. One person may need the touch of a hand. Another may need regular telephone calls to be assured that "somebody out there" remembers. Still another may need special visits from pastor and friends. The needs will vary from situation to situation and from person to person. Genuine caring not only will see to it that the rituals are performed but also will see that the *person* is cared for. The Dorothys may assume that others will provide this personal dimension, but that is not always a safe assumption. (We will discuss this further in our comments near the end of the chapter on the minister's role in caring.)

### Frank (pages 11–12)

We move on to Frank. How would you evaluate him as a caregiver? What descriptive name would you assign to him? Take time now to list the strengths and weaknesses that you have identified in the way in which he gives care.

We see Fearful Frank as a sensitive male who genuinely cares for Mary because of real feelings that he himself has experienced. Because of his own recent loss, he can identify with Mary's feelings of grief. This is not to say that he knows exactly how Mary feels—her grief is hers alone—but Frank is aware of the emotions that are involved with the death of a parent and wants to extend his sympathy to her. Frank is also gifted with a capacity to detach himself from this grief experience so that he doesn't so over-identify with Mary that he becomes a useless puddle of emotions.

There is a fine line, however, between overidentifying with someone's experience and backing away completely from sharing your own. Because of Frank's own feelings of being out of control when his father died, he assumes that sharing his grief experience may in some way trigger Mary to lose control also. Losing control is so uncomfortable for him that he wants to be sure not to "inflict" this on someone else. His own self-imposed virtue of "keeping it together" interferes with his ability to extend care to others. He is unwilling or unable to risk breaking down with Mary in a moment of shared grief.

As we said earlier, both detachment and control are necessary at times in caring, but, carried to an extreme, they may be interpreted as coldness and aloofness. Frank needs to become aware that his gifts of identification and feeling are equally important and can be balanced with detachment and control in order to bring about effective caring.

### Roger (page 12)

Let's turn our attention now to Roger. Identify some of his strengths and weaknesses in caregiving and give him an appropriate title.

Roger the Robot is a person who has always been interested in people and willing to help when he sensed their need, but he always felt that he should do it by the book. He was aware that acquiring the appropriate skills would aid him in communicating his care for others. In fact, he spent a considerable amount of time and energy developing these skills in college and therefore felt comfortable trying to initiate a caring conversation with Mary.

However, we get the feeling that Roger has not had much experience with people in actual life situations. Most of his skills have been learned and practiced in an academic setting, not with people experiencing pain and grief. His words come across as mechanical, and he is unable (although very willing) to communicate his genuine feelings to Mary. In some ways he is like Dorothy in sticking to the rules and somewhat like Frank in failing to communicate his true level of feeling.

On the one hand, Roger's level of energy and willingness to learn caring skills is admirable. But on the other hand, Roger is too much of a robot. His caring comes across as stiff and mechanical, because he becomes so caught up in the technique that his own personal nature and concern are not expressed. Later in this book we will be introducing you to skills in caring, but we want those skills to be expressed in ways that are *natural* for you and not imitations of us or others.

### Ruth (pages 12–13)

Our description of Ruth was fairly brief, but, as with the others, we invite you to give her a descriptive title and identify some strengths and weaknesses that you see in her manner of seeking to care for Mary.

Ruth might be called The Grapevine. She seems to be the first to hear news—good or bad—and has her own network for passing the word along. Her concern for Mary is genuine, and she wants to reach out in a helpful way. Her greatest strength lies in taking the initiative to get in touch with both Charles and Mary. The contact with their minister indicates her awareness that multiple resources are needed in times of loss. Unfortunately, the networking broke down with Charles. Ruth's timely contact with Mary demonstrates her willingness to extend herself to people in painful moments. Furthermore, she could share her own sense of identification with Mary's long ordeal. In the best of all possible worlds of caring, that identification would serve as an invitation to Mary to work through much of the pain she had suffered over the last months.

But, as is often the case, the strength has a flip side, which becomes a weakness if not guarded very carefully. Ruth's identification is so intense that she becomes focused on herself and loses sight of Mary and Mary's needs. So Ruth begins to do the very thing that we wish Mary had the opportunity to do: talk about her difficulties. It's too bad that Mary did not get the invitation from Ruth to do the same.

## Charles (page 13)

What descriptive title would you give to Charles? Think of the strengths and weaknesses that you see in his response to Mary.

Charles is a person whom you might call a workaholic. His strength lies in the immense dedication and energy he puts into carrying the major responsibility for all the programs of the church. In fact, our title for him is Overextended Minister. In this way he is very similar to Mary, with whom we began. She took sole responsibility for her mother's care; he takes responsibility for the church's care. They are two figures who seem to give unceasingly, serving as an inspiration to others to do likewise. Not only do they initiate, they follow through. Furthermore, carrying out their commitments does not require approval or appreciation from others. They simply do what needs to be done.

The flip side of this strength is that others are not given the opportunity, or even an invitation, to participate in the caring. Charles may want to take care of everything, but he can't. The incident with Mary is a prime example. He could not both lead the retreat and care for Mary during her time of grief. But because he had not acknowledged that such times would occur, no provision had been made for others to share in the caring. Not only does this neglect become a personal weakness for Charles but it results in an institutional weakness for the congregation's caring ministry. Had Charles focused his dedication and energy on enabling others to care, instead of assuming full responsibility himself, perhaps Mary would not have grieved alone. Super models, such as Charles, set themselves up for super failure sooner or later. That is why caring must be shared—for the well-being of all of us. And that is the way God intended us to live as a priesthood of all believers. We all are human, which means we are limited in our abilities. Therefore we are all called to share in this ministry of caring for each other.

### For Your Reflection and Devotional Thought

Throughout this chapter we have asked you to evaluate the strengths and weaknesses of the characters in our office scenario. Now we would like you to take a few moments to think about your own strengths and weaknesses in caring for others. This is a form of discipline we will encourage throughout your journey in caring. "Discipline" is in fact a theological term. The word literally means "discipling," or learning how to "follow in the Way." Jesus is a model in caring for us. His regular times of withdrawing for prayer and reflection on his ministry set an example for us in our caring. Such times are important for us in maintaining focus instead of becoming so scattered that we lose our effectiveness. Take time out to think about yourself in the same way that we have asked you to think about Mary, Joe, and the others. What are your strengths and weaknesses as a caregiver?

*Lord, I thank you for the gifts you have given me, but I confess that I am sometimes fearful of using them. Give me the courage to claim my strengths and the knowledge to use them responsibly. Help me also to be aware of my weaknesses and to learn from them. And finally, help me to recognize my own need to be cared for—both by others and by you. Amen.*

# 3

# Getting Started

The first two chapters have emphasized the importance of living out the caring that we receive through Jesus Christ. Those chapters focused on some examples from a situation in which many people were working hard to express their caring. Now we will look more intently into caring skills.

## Initiating the Relationship

Every relationship has to start somewhere, and many people leave that to chance. But a caring relationship calls for a certain amount of planning. For one thing, caring does not just happen. If we left it to chance, much caring would never take place. The person in need hesitates to express these needs openly at any given moment. The caregiver often misses subtle signals that help is needed. Because of this tendency to avoid uncomfortable situations caused by asking for or offering help, a certain amount of advance planning needs to take place in order to ensure a responsible level of effective care. We cannot leave it to chance. Thus, it is important to extend ourselves as caregivers in order to initiate the caring process. Just as God initiates grace to us, even though we may not even know we need it, so we are called to initiate care to others. The receiver of care will then be free, though not required, to respond to that offer of concern rather than having to ask for it. Initiating and planning do not mean controlling. The freedom of the recipient of care is an important dimension of such a relationship. The giver of care carries a responsibility to initiate, or invite, a person to talk about important issues, but there is an equally important responsibility to leave maneuvering room for the person to accept or reject the offer. This chapter focuses on the responsibilities involved in initiating a caring relationship.

When extending care to someone, it is important to know what the limits are. Every relationship has boundaries. For example, there are things you will do for a spouse that you won't do for a friend, and vice versa. When a student walks into a classroom, he or she knows that the teacher is the one in charge and that certain things are expected of each student. In other words, every relationship has a set of rules that are either stated or implied. One feature of a healthy relationship is that the partners have openly agreed on the rules. Unhealthy relationships are often shaky because no one knows what the boundaries are. Those involved don't know fully what to expect. A caring relationship, therefore, functions best if both giver and receiver are clear about what is taking place.

People don't tend to open up very well to strangers. After all, our society has shown us that a stranger can be either our enemy or our friend. We may even watch our family and friends closely at the beginning of a conversation to see what they are "up to" or what they want. The reason for this careful way of responding to each other lies in our fear of getting into something we can't handle. That's why it is important in your caring to let the person know clearly who you are and why you are there at that particular time. You might think of it as setting the stage or, in our terms, initiating the relationship. You are building a structure, a setting, or an atmosphere in which caring may take place. And it is as important for the person to know what you *don't* expect as to know what you *do* expect. The major means for accomplishing this task of initiation are threefold: gathering information about the person and the situation, defining yourself as a caregiver, and extending an invitation.

## Gathering Information

People generally don't like to walk into unfamiliar situations. This is just as true of caregivers, maybe even more so. When we are on our way into a sensitive situation, we want to know all that we can in advance. Such preparation serves several purposes. First, if we have advance information, we will feel more certain about what to expect. Our own sense of secure well-being is an important ingredient in a context for caring. If we are uncomfortable or uncertain about the situation, our anxiety becomes contagious and may well unsettle the person we have come to comfort, who now has *our* discomfort to deal with too.

Second, in our attempt to minimize our discomfort and that of the other person, we often tend to shy away from heavy issues. Our own dis-ease leads us to make sure that we *don't* talk about anything significant. This kind of insecurity leads to many conversations about the weather, followed by, "Hope to see you again soon." Both you and the person visited are well aware that the level of care given and received will not move beyond a cordial exchange. There can even be an unspoken agreement *not* to talk about uncomfortable issues. Neither expects the conversation to develop into an exploration of more sensitive feelings.

On the other hand, if we know about the situation into which we are going, we may not be as fearful about what is to be said. When visiting a person who is facing a terminal illness, we can anticipate that we will be talking about death. Having had time and opportunity to prepare ourselves for such a conversation, we are more likely to be able to handle it and even to be sure that the person is given an opportunity to describe some of the pain.

In addition to providing us with a level of security, gathering information also works to the advantage of the other person. When we know, for instance, that a certain man has recently lost a spouse by death, we go with the intention of helping him in very specific ways. He will receive care that we have thought about in advance. To know the name of his wife, for example, makes it easier to talk about her death. To know the nature of the illness, whether sudden or expected, gives added insight into his grief experience. If the death occurred after a long and torturous illness, there may be a sense of relief that you will understand if it is mentioned. On the other hand, if a family member was suddenly killed in an automobile accident, you can anticipate shock and disbelief as manifestations of the grief. Information about such things can often be obtained from a friend, pastor, nurse, or doctor. Gathering information enables the caring to be more personalized, assuring recipients that you care about them as individuals.

You may be asking whether this gathering of information borders on being nosy. The obvious answer is yes. However, one of the responsibilities of caregiving is being able to walk the thin line between what we *want* to know (curiosity) and what we *need* to know (relevant information). Visiting a person who has cancer, you may find yourself curious about many of the details of the disease and its process. Your conversation may then focus on these details instead of on the person. On the other hand, just knowing that a person has cancer doesn't tell you all you *need* to know. Knowing the location and extent of the disease enables you to understand the feelings with which the person is dealing. A helpful question to ask yourself when gathering information is, Do I need this information to help initiate this relationship or am I simply satisfying my curiosity?

Gathering information about the *timing* of your visit is also important. When planning to visit someone at home, you need to decide whether it would be okay just to drop in or whether telephoning first would be more appropriate. If you already know the person, then of course you can make a better decision. If you don't know the person, you can ask someone who does. For instance, when you are making a hospital visit, it is wise to check with the nurse about the patient's present condition and whether or not it is a good time for a visit. If all else fails, just ask the person. Often we are too cautious and hesitate to give the person who is being visited the opportunity to tell us what's best. In any case, remember that timing also includes *length* of visit. Routine caring visits in a hospital should not exceed ten minutes.

Remember Mary, described in chapters 1 and 2? She is a person in need of care. People who want to help are all around her. But look at what they did and didn't do in terms of this first step in initiating the relationship of helping. Joe certainly spent time thinking about what to do. In fact, he agonized over it. But all the thinking and preparing went on primarily within himself. He failed to gather any information about *Mary's* specific needs, so when he made his attempt to care, he felt frustrated. Dorothy, on the other hand, felt quite satisfied with what she did. But her ritualized response resulted in no more than general care, and Mary wound up neglected over the weekend. Frank assumed that Mary's feelings would be the same as his own. Consequently, he gave to her what *he* needed instead of finding out what *she* needed. Roger too had a preprogrammed style of assuming what was important. And Ruth wound up telling rather than listening.

A factor that all these people shared in common was the failure to gather information. Thus, a caring relationship characterized by *particular* care in a specific situation was not initiated.

## Defining Yourself

All of us live and function in a variety of roles daily. At the same time that you are functioning as a parent, you may also be functioning as a spouse, sibling, child, employee, club treasurer, and church visitor. Depending on your particular role in a given moment, you naturally speak to people in different ways. As a parent, you may tell your child to shape up. As a sibling, you may tease your sister about the time you caught her sneaking out of the house with her girlfriend. As an employee, you may become very friendly, anxious to please and equally anxious to make a sale. As a church visitor, you come as a representative of a larger group of people who share common beliefs and interests in being supportive to people in need.

Therefore, when you enter a room, the person being visited may wonder which role you are in and why you are there. Once you have identified your role, the boundaries are established for appropriate conversation. For example, one day when a chaplain we know introduced himself to a hospital patient as "Dr. Jones," the patient began to undress for an examination! He hastily explained that he was a minister, not a physician.

When you get right down to it, defining yourself simply means that you tell the person who you are and why you have come. You may know the person well and even have played many rounds of golf together. However, to say, "Jack, I've heard that you are having a hard time lately, and I want you to know that I care," tells Jack clearly that you're more concerned about *him* than the last golf game. Once you have defined yourself to Jack at this point as a care-giver (as well as his golf buddy), he has the choice of responding to either role.

Ministers have to deal with this all the time. When the pastor appears at the door, a church member wonders if this visit is to inquire about an absence from church, to urge participation on a committee, or to push for a larger pledge. When the pastor says, "I came by to see how things have been since your mother died," the wondering ceases and the visiting can really begin.

Some friendships allow the flexibility for either party to change roles according to their needs. For instance, in a lunch conversation with a close friend, one could say, after some friendly chitchat, "I'm so glad we could get together today, because I have a problem that I need to talk to you about. Can we take a little time to sort it through?" This is a situation in which the one who needs some care feels free to ask the other to take on another role too; that is, to re-define the relationship. One friend has become the "person in need" and the other has become the "caregiver." The roles have changed temporarily, but the friendship remains intact.

The change of roles in such a friendship could occur at the initiative of the other friend, who might say, "You look sort of troubled today. Feel like talking about it?" Here again, a redefinition takes place. One friend has declared willingness to become a care-giver to the other.

You may think we are making a big deal out of this business of defining yourself, but it really makes a difference in caring situations. Sadly enough, rela-tionships in which people feel free to ask each other to change roles are few and far between. This is par-ticularly true when we think about asking someone to care for us. Many of us have been raised to avoid making someone else feel uncomfortable. That trans-lates into "Don't tell other people about your troubles." As you realize this, it is all the more important for you as the caretaker to *take the initiative* in defining yourself as one who has come prepared and willing to care. Then the one in need of care is relieved of worrying about whether or not to unload, because the caregiver has already shown a willingness to "take it."

Let's go back to Mary, from chapters 1 and 2. The death of her mother threw her fellow workers into something of a role crisis. They knew how to be the recipient of her attention, and they knew how to work with her in accomplishing their various responsibilities in the office. But who were they to be in this situation? What role should they assume with her now? They wanted to be caregivers but were limited in their effectiveness. Let's explore the ways in which some of them defined themselves.

Joe's frustration interfered with his defining himself at all as a caregiver. Dorothy chose a role that, although comfortable for her, kept her at a distance from Mary. The flowers were a caring gesture, and such symbols are important. But Dorothy could have added a dimension to her caring by making personal contact. Mary's minister was torn in knowing what to do when he called her. His various roles as minister called on him to be faithful to his commitments for the retreat and to be a caregiver to Mary. The external circumstances created an internal conflict of roles, limiting the caring that Mary would receive.

Definition of role in a caring situation involves some very personal issues. We hope that you will do some careful thinking about who you are and who you want to be to people in need of care. An exercise at the end of this chapter will give you an opportunity to try out some of these roles. But remember, we aren't trying to get you to play a role. We are looking for ways to help you to be yourself in caring situations.

Remember that in defining yourself you must be

conscious of who you are in relationship to God and to others. The process of discovering the roles that you may play in caring for others will involve opening yourself to the strength that comes from those relationships, especially with God. We will be offering suggestions in the last chapter about ways to nurture your relationships with God and others in order to share our caring.

## Extending an Invitation

"Extending an invitation" isn't the same thing as a pulpit call, but we have deliberately chosen this term. There is a connection. You, the visitor, have the opportunity to "invite" a person to talk about some sensitive issues. This is similar to the invitation that God extends to each of us in the form of grace.

God's grace comes to us whether we ask for it or not. Yet, when we experience it, it is always in a form that gives us a choice. We can say no. And often we do. Sometimes the goodness that is offered to us by God, or by various persons, is more than we can stand in a given moment. Take forgiveness as an example. When a child has done something wrong and is feeling guilty, words of comfort are not always helpful. As a parent I can tell my daughter "It's all right," but that doesn't necessarily convince her. She needs to feel bad a while longer. My forgiveness, or grace, is something that she is not ready for at that moment.

Or consider a man who has been told he has cancer. A visitor comes into the room and invites him to talk about his fears. That invitation is grace-full. It says that the man may, if he wishes, talk about all the feelings that come when that dread word—cancer— is pronounced. But he isn't ready to talk about it yet. He may shake his head, saying, "Thanks—but no, thanks." Part of his thankfulness may be that the visitor didn't, in some way, *demand* that he talk about his fears.

God's grace is much like that. We are invited to confess that we are sinners. We are also invited to admit that we aren't as in control of our lives as we would like to be, but we are assured that we are still loved. We aren't always ready or willing to admit such things about ourselves. God knocks, and we are invited to respond, but God doesn't beat the door down. God gives us the freedom to decide whether and when we wish to respond to that grace.

When you are initiating a caring relationship, you need to extend such an invitation. The message should be clear that you are available, but you demand nothing in response. You aren't going to judge your own worth or that of the other person by whether the invitation is accepted or not. Caring is a gift, not a summons. It is an invitation, not a demand. It is a covenant, not a contract.

What, then, do you say when you enter Jack's room? The principle may sound simple, but it is not always easy to do. Basically, it means that early in the conversation you make it OK to talk about uncomfortable topics. You also give freedom not to do so. You might say, "Jack, I know that you have some serious surgery coming up. If you'd like to talk about it, I'm ready to listen." Exactly what you say will vary according to the relationship and the situation, but the message that you deliver remains the same.

An invitation properly extended, of course, presumes the first two ingredients that we have discussed in the process of initiating a relationship. When you invite someone and genuinely want a response, you try in advance to learn as much about the person as you can. After all, if you know the particular things he or she likes, the situations that would produce discomfort, the subjects that are most interesting, then you can express your invitation in such a way that the person knows enough to take you seriously. You have done your homework (gathered information), so your invitation is not an idle one.

Further, in planning your invitation, you can make some choices about how to use your own attributes. What do you want the person to know about you that will make it easier for him or her to respond to your invitation? This is what we mean by defining yourself. You introduce yourself in such a way that it becomes comfortable for the person to respond.

Your invitation, then, is built on the elements of gathering information and defining yourself carefully. Those ingredients are essential to an invitation that is extended effectively. But it is equally important that the invitation be gracious enough that a person will not be made to feel guilty for not accepting. The height of graciousness lies in the ability of the inviter to make it possible for the invited either to accept or to refuse and still feel cared for and accepted.

Again, recall the characters in chapters 1 and 2. Joe, Dorothy, and Frank failed to extend invitations altogether. Roger tried, and we will comment on that in the next chapter. Ruth used her visit with Mary to create an invitation to herself to talk to Mary about her *own* problems.

Taking the initiative to extend an invitation moves away from the more technical aspects of caring into the sphere of art. Our personality begins to weave the information we have gathered and our perception of what role will be most helpful into a tapestry of caring that is tailor-made for the person in need. Once this artistic invitation is extended, we are prepared to move into the task of nurturing the caring relationship.

Initiating a caring relationship is difficult to learn just by reading. So we would like to recommend that you experiment a bit with initiating one of your own. The following exercise can be done with one other person or, even better, with groups of people who are learning to improve their skills. You can even do it alone, using your imagination. Please try it. After the first moment or two of feeling awkward, we think you will find it useful.


## Initiating Exercise

We will assume that there are two participants in this exercise. If more are involved, divide into groups of three or four. Two persons will carry on a conversation and the other(s) will observe.

One participant, A, assumes the role of a person in need. Make it simple in terms of the circumstances: You are a person who has recently suffered the loss of someone by death, but don't make it too complicated. The second participant, B, takes the role of caregiver. In this exercise, assume that you don't know the person very well on whom you are calling.

B makes a call at the home of A. In your initiating, be conscious of the three dimensions discussed in this chapter. Then the two of you should engage in a brief conversation. A minute or two is plenty. Then stop and reflect on what happened.

Participant A should be the first person to evaluate the exchange. Then B and the observers (if any) can share their views on how the relationship was initiated. Some of A's evaluative comments could include the following:

1. When you were introducing yourself, I felt ———.
2. Your primary interest in coming to see me seemed to be ———.
3. My initial response to you was ———, but I was too polite to say it.

Try the exercise again. Have each person try the role of visitor and be evaluated at least two different times. When you are in the role of visitor, try not to argue with the evaluative comments or explain why you did what you did. Just listen. After all, you are learning how your introduction is received by others, and you won't have a chance for rebuttal in the real situation. You may ask for further clarification about what your evaluators mean. Your job, though, during this evaluation period, is to *listen* and to *learn.*

## For Your Reflection and Devotional Thought

Read Luke 10:25–37 and Luke 19:1–10.

Remember early in this chapter we referred to God's grace, which is extended to us whether we ask for it or not. Often we are too fearful or unaware openly to admit our need for help. Therefore God often comes to us instead of waiting for us to develop the courage or the insight to ask. The story of the Good Samaritan is helpful in illustrating the importance of initiating. The man who had been beaten was readily observable, but several people passed him by. The Samaritan, who was the least likely to help, did so. Zacchaeus is also a helpful illustration of a person whose need was not so evident. Yet Jesus recognized the need and stopped and called out to him.

Take a few minutes to think about the presence of God's grace in your own life. What were the circumstances? Did you experience God's grace directly or through another person? What are some of the ways that you would like to extend that grace to others?

It is our belief that God's grace nurtures us, in part, so that we may become the initiators of that care to others. If we are aware of the many ways God's grace comes to us, then we are both eager and energized to share that caring with others. This chapter is an invitation to you to participate actively and willingly in initiating caring for people in need so that they may be willing recipients of God's grace.

*Gracious and grace-full God, thank you for the times you have extended yourself to me before I even knew of my need. Give me the insight and the courage to become one who shares that grace with others in ways that are both skillful and caring. Amen.*

# 4

# Nurturing
# the Relationship

Listening is a major skill that is involved in nurturing a relationship once it has been initiated. It may well be the most important skill we can learn for communicating our depth of caring.

To nurture any relationship successfully, *all* parties concerned must utilize the elements of good communication. Many times, neither party knows what those elements are. But if you want to create a good relationship, it is important to devote some attention to understanding what's happening when two persons communicate.

Too many people assume that communication means sending a message. Therefore they spend a great deal of time and energy finding just the right words and just the right vehicle for delivering their message effectively. But ironically, it turns out that our message of caring is delivered best by receiving words *from* the other person. In other words, nurturing a caring relationship demands that we learn to listen.

## The Importance of Listening

Listening communicates the message that we care enough to take the time to let a person say all that matters. We don't rush. We don't interrupt. We don't say the person is wrong. We just listen. The result of this listening is that we learn about the person and communicate our acceptance of him or her as a valuable human being. In a very real sense, we "tell" that person we care, not with our mouths but with our ears. We deliver our message of care by *receiving* what the person wishes to tell us.

This assertion may sound like psychological malarkey, but it's just good common sense. If another person gets the message that we are interested, that person feels more comfortable with us and will risk sharing with us. It's not guaranteed, but it is more likely. If we spend more time listening than talking, the communication is clear. It says, "I am interested in you. You matter!"

In the following conversation, Joyce demonstrates some important listening skills in initiating a relationship of caring with Nancy. But notice that she also misses an important opportunity.

During a committee meeting one evening, Joyce had noticed that Nancy seemed preoccupied and not involved in the discussion. In fact, she had almost seemed teary at times. Joyce had also heard from several dependable sources that Nancy's son, George, had been involved in some trouble at school. As the meeting ended, Joyce took a deep breath and decided to initiate a conversation with Nancy.

As everyone was leaving, Joyce walked with Nancy to her car, chatting about the various issues that had been discussed. When they reached the car, Joyce looked around to make sure no one else was standing nearby and then made her big move.

JOYCE:  Nancy, I couldn't help noticing that you seemed upset during the meeting. I just want you to know that I care about you, and if you'd like to talk, we could go get a cup of coffee.

NANCY  *(sighs):* Thanks, Joyce. I am feeling upset, and maybe we could go get that cup of coffee. . . . *(Then, later, at the restaurant)* Joyce, I really do appreciate your noticing and taking the time to talk with me. It's so hard sometimes to tell someone about the things that matter to you most, especially when you aren't sure people will understand.

JOYCE: Well, I did notice that you seemed upset. *(There is a period of uncomfortable silence, during which Nancy fumbles with her coffee cup, wrings her napkin, and keeps her head down. Several times she starts to say something like "It's so hard . . ." or "I don't know where to begin" or "It's such a big mess," but the words just don't come.)*

JOYCE *(uncomfortable with the silence):* Well, I've heard about the problems that George is having at school. It must be just terrible for you to be having to worry about all that. It would just kill me! How on earth are you able to cope with it all? I know that I would just want to die from embarrassment.

NANCY: Well, I have been upset about George *(she puts her head in her hands),* but that's not the worst of it. It's just so hard. . . . *(She starts to cry.)*

JOYCE *(feeling very uncomfortable with Nancy's tears):* Oh, please don't be upset. It can't really be all that bad. Let me tell you about the time that . . . *(She launches into a long story about her most embarrassing moment with her own child.)*

NANCY *(looking more and more frustrated):* Well, thank you, Joyce, for the cup of coffee. It was really sweet of you to suggest this, but I really have to go now.

JOYCE *(startled and fearful that she hasn't been helpful enough):* Oh, Nancy, maybe the

best thing is to just get George out of that
school. There are probably some bad in-
fluences for him there.

The next day Joyce bumped into Helen, a mutual
friend, at the grocery store. Helen said, "Joyce, have
you heard? Nancy is getting a divorce!" Joyce stared
at her in amazement. She had just been with Nancy
the night before. How could she have missed knowing that?

While this situation ended differently from the
way Joyce expected, we do commend her for the
skillful way in which she *initiated* the relationship
with Nancy. She demonstrated all the criteria discussed in the previous chapter. From what she had
heard previously and what she saw now, Joyce concluded that Nancy was someone in need of care
*(gathering information)*. She waited for an appropriate time, when Nancy was alone, to *define herself* as
someone who had noticed Nancy's distress, could
move out of her role as committee member, and was
willing to offer care. Not only was she willing, she
actually *extended an invitation* to Nancy by specifically offering an opportunity to talk. And Nancy was
receptive to the invitation. She took her up on it. So
far, so good.

But then comes the next step—nurturing the relationship. Once the relationship has been initiated,
listening skills are needed to nurture it. Listening
may not seem to be much of a skill, because it seems
passive and not active. When we care for someone,
we want to be "doing" something. But most of us will
find that just listening is truly an active skill, because
to listen and not open our mouths is very difficult.
Not to interject our own feelings or opinions calls for
a great deal of self-control. We actively need to re-
strain ourselves from talking as we listen. And when
we do say something, it should not add to or expand
what the other person has said. Rather, it should be

an attempt to clarify or confirm what has already been said.

If listening is important, let us remember that *not listening also communicates.* If we constantly monopolize the conversation, the message gets through that the other person doesn't really matter. By not listening, we communicate what is most important to us rather than indicating that we want to know what is most important to the other. So when a person doesn't respond positively to our telling her or him how much we care, it may well be because we did not listen and demonstrate *genuine* caring for her or his concerns.

If you are ready to exercise this vital element of self-control, you are ready to focus on the task of nurturing the caring relationship. The conversation between Joyce and Nancy will be used to demonstrate how listening skills can be developed. Then at the conclusion of the chapter there will be an opportunity to work with another conversation to practice the skills discussed.

## Listening for the Words

Listening is the process through which you learn about the person and his or her situation. Here are some important clues to help in the development of this discipline.

First, listen to the *choice* of words that the person uses. What does the vocabulary tell you? Are the words logical or do they seem to be emotionally loaded? Do they sound scholarly or practical and down-to-earth? Are the sentences complete or are there many sentence fragments? Do the words make sense to you or do you find yourself working very hard to figure out their meaning? Notice in our example that Nancy tended to use phrases rather than long, involved sentences. As she continued talking, her words revealed strong feelings, such as "upset," "so hard," and "mess." Notice too that she chose down-to-earth vocabulary, like "mess," rather than more scholarly terms, like "turmoil."

Second, when you are listening for the choice of words, it is also important to listen for *repetition.* Are some words or phrases being used again and again? Is there some particular word or phrase to which the conversation keeps returning? You will notice throughout this book that certain words and ideas are repeated. That is done because we think they are important. The same is true with a person telling you about problems. Without realizing it, he or she will repeat the things that are most important. All you need to do is listen for that repetition.

By listening for the words and for the repetition, you may notice a *theme* developing in what the person is saying. What continuous thread keeps running through the conversation? If you were going to write one or two paragraphs to summarize that theme, what would you say? Try to organize in your own mind, and in your own words, what the person has told you.

Nancy, for instance, in her conversation with Joyce manifested a troubled theme, but she was not specific about it. She told Joyce of her discomfort in talking about it without saying what "it" was. Joyce was on target in picking up the theme that Nancy was troubled, but she leaped too quickly to assume that she knew what the trouble was. She concluded that Nancy's problem with her son at school was the primary reason for Nancy's distress, so Joyce proceeded with that subject. Part of the discipline of listening lies in allowing time for the person to develop his or her own theme. Too often we tend to cut the other person off with our preliminary assumptions. Even if we have been good at gathering information, we still need to listen for answers to three important questions. First, is our information correct and accurate? Second, even if the information is correct, is this what the person really wants to talk about *now?* Third, if our information is correct, and the person wants to talk about it now, what are that person's particular feelings and experience?

Remember that our job is to listen, not to assure the other person that we already know what is going on. Such assurance cuts a person off instead of encouraging further talk. It is *their talking* and *our listening* that is needed at this point in order to nurture the relationship.

### Listening for the Feelings

There is, however, more to what a person says than the words. Feelings lie behind words. And the feelings will often clarify what the words mean. Think of the number of times each day that you greet someone with the words, "How are you?" Have you ever noticed the different ways in which the person can give the expected reply, "Fine"? Some say it with genuine cheerfulness. Others utter it in a monotone, offering the ritual reply and no more. Someone else may answer with a touch of sarcasm, while another may sound so tired that the word and the tone of voice seem at absolute odds with each other.

When you are caring for someone, you have the responsibility to listen to more than the person's words. Listen to the feelings that become evident through the tone of voice. Do the words *sound* angry, sad, enthusiastic, discouraged, tired? Does the tone vary from one issue to the other? Are there mixed messages when you listen to both the words and the tone of voice? Do they seem to be in conflict with each other?

Summarize all these observations in your mind. Ask yourself, What has this person really communicated to me? It is not possible for us to illustrate the tones of voice in the conversation between Joyce and Nancy, but Nancy's "sigh" is one indication of some feeling behind the words. Perhaps her sigh is communicating a sense of tiredness, resignation, or desperation. Wondering what the true feeling is will enable you to focus even more consciously on the task of listening as the conversation continues.

## Watching for What Is Said

There is more to listening than listening! It also includes *watching*. You need to listen with your eyes as well as your ears! Increased attention has been given in recent years to what is called non-verbal communication. All of us literally talk with our bodies. Posture, facial expressions, movement of the hands, glances of the eyes—all of these work to confirm or to contradict what we are saying with our mouths. One simple example lies in what we mean when we say of someone that she talks with her hands. As that person talks, there are continual gestures. The gestures tell you which points are more important than others. Some of the movements give you the sense of calmness, others of excitement, others of strong emphasis. If the hands were tied down, the ability to communicate would be seriously affected. Often when people are uncomfortable, they look for something to do with their hands. Nancy fumbled with her coffee cup and wrung her napkin. Other people might pick at a fingernail or continually put their hands in and out of their pockets.

Watch for nonverbal communication as you listen. If Jim says, "I am very glad to see you" but continues to look at his desk, shuffling papers, you may wonder whether to believe the words or his very visible preoccupation with his work. Don't worry about how to respond to this situation right now. We'll deal with that later. At this point, concentrate on *noticing* behavior and becoming aware of what happens nonverbally.

Here are a few specific things to note:

1. Does the person look relaxed or tense? What do you notice about his or her posture in the chair? Slouched? Rigid? Does the person lean forward with interest or sit back with a reserved or cautious appearance?

2. What messages do you receive from the person's eyes? Behavioral specialists tell us the eyes don't lie. Do they seem bright and interested or dull and withdrawn? Humorous? Suspicious? Is there direct eye contact?

3. What kind of movement do you notice? Does the person sit immobile or is there nervous shifting around in the chair? Are there frequent glances at the clock or a watch? Do you notice nail-biting or wringing of hands?

Think back again to the conversation between Joyce and Nancy. Joyce began her listening with her observations of Nancy during the meeting. Remember her noting that Nancy looked preoccupied and almost teary at times. That observation led Joyce to begin pulling together the information that she already had about Nancy and decide to make herself available to listen even more. Later, in the restaurant, Nancy gave further clues to her feelings by fumbling with her coffee cup, wringing her hands, and keeping her head down. All these messages were there for Joyce to gain further insight into Nancy's distress.

## Putting It All Together

Now put it all together, and what do you have? Do you get clear, consistent messages from your visit or do they appear muddled and mixed? Think about the words you have heard, the feelings you sensed, and the behavior you observed. Is there continuity in the themes that come from these three dimensions of communication? Or do you notice that words, feelings, and behavior don't seem to fit together? This is a critical time for reflection. It is very important for you to become aware of all the dimensions involved in listening before you respond.

Here is a list of the messages Nancy delivered:

1. Words: "upset," "so hard," "things that matter," "big mess"
2. Feelings: distressed, upset, depressed, sad
3. Behavior: teary, fumbling with hands, head down

In this situation, all these dimensions are consistent with one another, but this doesn't happen in every case. Inconsistency alerts us to the need for further exploration. Consistency tempts us to race into assumptions that may or may not be true. Nancy's consistent messages led Joyce into the trap of thinking that she knew the problem. Consequently, a situation developed in which she failed to exercise properly the discipline of responding.

## The Discipline of Responding

If you have initiated the relationship well by gathering information, defining yourself, and extending an invitation, you have placed yourself in an excellent position to hear the person's concerns in a genuinely helpful way. Now, having heard those expressions, you have the opportunity to respond in a caring way. Whether or not you will be helpful depends on the manner in which you respond.

One of the greatest temptations for us as caregivers is the belief that we have to *do* something for those in need. We want to provide them with relief from their discomfort. That is the trap into which Joyce fell in our earlier example. Out of her own need to ease Nancy's pain, she assured her that things weren't "all that bad" before she even knew what those things were. She assumed that she knew what was wrong and, without allowing Nancy to tell the *whole* story, began to make suggestions based on her faulty perceptions.

In the transition from listening to responding, your task is to check it out with the person to make sure that what you have heard is not only accurate but complete. The technical term for checking it out is *reflection.* Like a good mirror, you reflect back to the other person the images or messages you have received. You have probably heard all sorts of jokes about counselors who simply repeat back what the client has said. Roger, in chapter 1, used this technique in responding to Mary. That stereotype is an exaggeration of what we are going to ask you to work on. The art of reflection lies in your being able to tell the person, *without using the same words,* what you have heard. You function as a mirror, not as a tape recorder. The image in a mirror, remember, is not really the same, but it looks the same. The image is recognizable. In the same way, the words you use are not merely a recorded playback but a *reflection* of what you have heard, rephrased. The thoughts and feelings are recognizable.

This process of reflection is designed to ensure that you have heard correctly and that the person *knows* that he or she has been heard accurately. Our goal is that the person will say to you in some way, "You really *do* understand!" And, of course, the feeling of being understood is one of the ultimate experiences of feeling cared for. When a person feels understood, that person *knows* someone is responding fully.

Our task, then, is to develop the skills that allow us to assure the person that she or he has been heard. And if we have not heard correctly, it is important to assure the person that we *want* to understand.

### Repeating What You Have Heard and Seen

There are several steps in the process of reflection. The first one is obvious in the name of the technique. You are to reflect, not add to, what the person has said. In other words, simply repeat what you have heard and seen without second-guessing where you think the person is going. If you constantly try to read the person's mind, anticipating where she or he is going next, you lose your ability to concentrate on what the person is saying at that moment. You need to avoid a very natural reaction—assuming that you already know what another person thinks, feels, and wants. You may think you know, but you can't be sure. Everyone's experience is unique. Even if you know the circumstances and have experienced something similar, you still don't know the person's particular perspective in a given situation. It's up to the person to tell you, not for you to tell the person!

Here is the critical point at which Joyce failed Nancy. In her own discomfort at Nancy's slowness in saying what was the matter, Joyce jumped into her assumptions. Her vocabulary at this point tells it all. "I've heard about . . ."; "It must be . . ."; "It would. . . ." And then Joyce moves on, without checking for clarification, to say, "How on earth are you able . . . ?" Nancy was left misunderstood and with no invitation to clarify what was really going on.

### Developing the Vocabulary of Listening

The art of reflecting is strengthened by the development of a vocabulary that is more conducive to reflecting than to advising. Once you have learned to be more humble (such as restraining yourself when tempted to mind-read), you can further consolidate your skill by developing a vocabulary that supports you in your responsiveness. Most of this approach requires that you begin your sentences in ways that indicate you are *attempting* to understand and that you are open to being corrected. Phrases such as "It sounds like . . ." or "I get the impression that . . ." are typical of what we are attempting to describe. Select phrases that sound natural for *you*. Roger, in chapter 1, made the mistake of using learned jargon instead of developing his own vocabulary for communicating his desire to understand and learn more. Avoid at all costs picking up expressions that are more lengthy and complex than your usual speech patterns. As you begin to use appropriate reflective phrases, you will find that you are better able to hear what is *actually* said rather than making assumptions about what people have said to you. Disciplined responses help you control yourself.

## Communicating Nonverbally as Well

Remember Joe in chapter 1? He reached out and touched Mary, almost unconsciously, when he couldn't think of anything else to do. For Joe that may not have seemed to be very much. But that can be one of the most meaningful ways of sharing our caring. There are many times when words are not adequate for what we want to say. A gentle touch or a hug is concrete indication of the message "I care." When our words are preceded by or accompanied by touch, our concern often is communicated more clearly. Sometimes a touch without any words provides a gentle acceptance that says, "You don't have to say anything, and neither do I. But we can be together in the midst of all this." It is one more indication that our presence is real.

Touch is very personal, and it is very important that we not be pushy with our touching. If someone is uncomfortable with our reaching out in this way, he or she will usually make it clear. So even as we need to have touching in our repertoire of caring, we need to be discriminating in our use of it.

Allowing interludes of silence can be another effective nonverbal means of sharing our caring. Silences give troubled persons a time to reflect and decide just how much of themselves and their problem they wish to reveal. This is a very crucial point in any caring relationship. It's a clear test of who is in control. If you jump in and take over the conversation, you have just lost the opportunity to listen, the roles are reversed, and the person who may need to open up decides instead that it's better to close down. This is what happened between Nancy and Joyce.

How could Joyce have been a better listener? What could she have said (or not said) in response to Nancy? First of all, there is no one right answer. Several responses could be helpful and effective in showing Nancy that Joyce cared and wanted to listen.

Joyce was doing just great up to the "big silence." Then she, like so many of us, grew uncomfortable and felt the need to say something, anything, just to fill the gap. This will be one of your greatest challenges—overcoming the urge to break a silence. There is no easy way to accomplish this (and biting your tongue can be painful!). You just need to learn to endure.

The first thing Joyce could have done during the big silence was just to sit there and be quiet. If after several minutes there was still no response from Nancy, there were several ways to show care without taking control.

If Nancy became teary and began to cry, Joyce could have gently offered her a tissue.

If Nancy continued to keep her head bowed without speaking, Joyce could gently touch her on her arm, saying something like, "I'm sorry that you're hurting" or "I'm sorry this is such a difficult time for you."

If Nancy continued to be noncommunicative and

more upset, Joyce could suggest that they go somewhere more private, perhaps one of their homes.

Had Joyce been more in control of her verbal and nonverbal responses, the conversation might have turned out this way:

During the period of uncomfortable silence, Joyce heard Nancy start to say such things as, "It's so hard . . ."; "I don't know where to begin . . ."; "It's such a big mess."

JOYCE  *(after several minutes of silence, reaching over the table and touching Nancy gently on the arm):* You really seem to be struggling with some painful things.

NANCY: Well, I've been upset about a lot of things lately. *(Starts to cry.)* It's just too much.

JOYCE: It sounds like you're feeling pretty overwhelmed. *(Hands Nancy a tissue.)*

NANCY: Yes, that's right. But I've got to start getting my life together. *(Looks at Joyce as if she is both eager and afraid to talk.)* Are you sure you're ready to hear all this?

JOYCE  *(with fear and trepidation):* Yes, Nancy, that's why I'm here.

Nancy then begins to tell about the problems with her marriage, her child, etc. We can't promise that things will always go this smoothly if you follow these guidelines on listening. However, using these skills will increase the likelihood that your caring will be clearly perceived.

## An Exercise to Check Your Listening Skills

The following scenario will give you an opportunity to check your own reflective listening skills. This exercise can be done by you alone, but it may be more helpful with a friend. After the introductory paragraph about the situation, there will be state-

ments made by John, the person to whom you will be
listening. After John speaks, you are invited to suggest a response that communicates your understanding and encourages him to continue. Don't worry if
his next statement doesn't seem to follow. After all,
we don't know what you are going to say!

If someone else is joining you in the exercise, each
of you could write down your own responses. Then
you can compare your thoughts as an opportunity to
learn from each other. We will then suggest some
responses ourselves, but you should not assume that
there is only one right answer. There are many ways
in which we can manifest our caring and thus nurture a relationship.

Our saga begins with John and Bill, who met at
church three years ago when Bill and his family
moved to town and joined that congregation. The
two men quickly discovered a common love for golf
and have played almost weekly for over two years.
Both men use this time for relaxation and seldom
have discussed either business or personal matters.
Yet there is real warmth between them.

On this particular day on the course, John's game
seemed to be a bit off. Bill noticed that John seemed
less jovial than usual, but they had still exchanged a
few jokes as the afternoon wore on. After a frustrat-
ing putt on the fourteenth hole and a slice off the
fifteenth, John jammed his wood into the bag, declar-
ing, "It just seems nothing is going right in my life
right now!"

BILL:   Gosh, John, I don't think I've ever heard
        you that upset about a few bad shots.
JOHN:   Well, I've never been this upset before!
YOU:    *(What would you say if you were in Bill's
        spot at this point?)* [Response 1]
JOHN:   Well, of course it's more than just the golf
        game. I wish that all I had to deal with was
        straightening out a few iron shots.

YOU: [Response 2]

JOHN: I really can't believe it. I have been with this company for fifteen years. They promoted me; they encouraged me; they always commented on the bright future I had with them. And now, out of the blue, they tell me I have to take an early retirement. It just doesn't make sense. *(He shakes his head and walks on toward the next tee.)*

YOU: [Response 3]

JOHN: Thanks, Bill. I know you are trying to be helpful, but I don't think there is anything that *anybody* can do. It's my problem, and I'll have to carry it alone.

YOU: [Response 4]

Now that you have had a chance to propose a few responses, what do you think? If you were John, how would you respond to your responses?

Here are a few questions to help you evaluate yourself.

1. Did you stick with reflecting what John actually said instead of trying to add to it?
2. Did you pick up on the words that John was using and try to stick to words of the same emotional power?
3. Did you try to respond to John's actions as well as his words and feeling?
4. Did you find yourself focusing on attacking the company instead of listening to John's feelings?

John is struggling with a major issue. He is preoccupied and still stunned by the news that he has heard. You can pick up on those feelings by his vocabulary of "I really can't believe it" and "It just doesn't make sense."

Here are a few suggested responses that could have been made. Look them over, compare them with your own, and think about or discuss the strengths and weaknesses of each.

*Response 1:* "It sounds like you're dealing with a lot more than your golf game" *or* "John, we can forget the golf game if you have some pretty heavy stuff eating at you. Let's go somewhere and talk."

*Response 2:* "You're making noises like there is something pretty major going on in your life" *or* "Working on your golf game sounds pretty simple compared to whatever you are wrestling with."

*Response 3:* "So you have been going along with full assurance that everything was just fine and then this news comes like a bolt out of the blue" *or* "That's an incredible shock, especially when you had no reason to expect anything as radical as having to give up your job."

*Response 4:* "It's true that I can't change the situation at work for you, John, but I can sure let you know that I hear your hurting, and I want to be supportive" *or* "This is bound to leave you feeling alone, but I hope you won't shut us all off and wind up being lonely as well."

Continue to think about how to listen as we move into our next chapter, in which we deal with situations that may require more than listening.

### For Your Reflection and Devotional Thought

Read Psalms 22 and 88.

As you read these psalms, notice the power of the emotion that is being expressed. There is despair, anger, grief. But notice also the freedom with which the writer shares those feelings. It is as if there is sure and certain knowledge that the intensity is being heard and understood. Take some time to remember the occasions on which you appreciated being heard and understood without fearing that the listener would eventually give you some advice or encourage you "not to feel that way." Also take some time to think about God's gifts to you that enable you to stay with people in their times of discomfort and suffering.

*Gracious and understanding God, hear my prayer and give me the insight and strength really to hear the prayers of others in pain, in joy, in anger. May your understanding be reflected in my willingness to hear anything. May your peace be shared through me with those who yearn to be comforted and understood. Amen.*

# 5

# Self-knowledge
# and Responding to Loss

In working on your skills of listening, you have
learned to communicate your understanding in a
way that encourages an ongoing conversation. But
just as you are beginning to feel good about keeping
your mouth shut, the person asks you what he or she
ought to *do* about the situation. Now what? The person really wants you to say something. Suddenly you
feel caught in the bind of needing to maintain a listening posture and wanting to respond to the re-
quest. How can you be the most helpful?

The first inclination is to think, Well, if *I* were in
your shoes, I would . . . That inclination is to be
commended—as long as you don't say it out loud.

Your desire to do so is a reflection of your genuine
interest in the person and your attempt to understand his or her struggle. However, your desire also
comes from your need to "fix things." When we
*think* we understand, all too often we move quickly
toward a solution. Actually, offering a solution may
cut off the major help we can provide—the willingness to stay with the person while he or she works on
the problem.

It is important that you know three things in attempting to care effectively:

1. Knowledge of the person and the situation
2. Knowledge of your self

3. Knowledge of normal human development and experiences in the grief process

Knowledge about the other person and the situation is gained from gathering information and reflective listening, as described earlier. We focus in this chapter on the second and third kinds of knowledge.

## Self-knowledge

The emphasis to this point on listening to others may lead you to believe that caring focuses almost exclusively on the other person. However, it is almost equally important that you have a growing understanding of yourself. Why? Because one of your responsibilities in caring is being able to distinguish your own problems and solutions from those of the other person.

This second kind of knowledge involves knowing your strengths and weaknesses and perceptions of the world. Your own life experiences often leave you insensitive in some situations and vulnerable in others. For instance, if you have a parent who died of cancer, you may assume that the feelings of another person facing the loss of a family member by cancer are the same as your own. On the other hand, if you have never experienced the death of a child, you may feel sadness, but you won't know the unique intensity of that grief or special consequences that often surround it. Let's follow these two examples in a little more detail.

Tom is a banker. His mother died of cancer when he was getting his M.B.A. degree. His mother and father, out of a desire to protect Tom from the pain of her impending death, told him very little about the seriousness of her illness. Thus, in many ways the news of her death was a shock to him. In the years following, Tom wondered from time to time about what her death had been like, how long his mother and father had known, and why they had not told him more. For him, the death was almost unreal because of the lack of information given to him beforehand.

One day, while making hospital calls on behalf of his church, Tom visited a woman suffering in the final stages of cancer. Upon entering the room, Tom became a bit faint and found himself flooded with all sorts of feelings and questions. Was this the way his mother had looked? What would she have wanted him to say if he had been able to visit her? At the same time, he was aware of wanting to leave the room because of all the painful memories that were generated by seeing this woman. As a result, he left the room rather quickly, knowing that he was unable to be genuinely responsive to her needs. He realized that this visit had focused more on himself than on the woman in the hospital bed.

Later, when talking with his pastor about this encounter, Tom was aware of two things. First, he had finally been able to get in touch with all the unresolved feelings related to his mother's death that were still with him. As a result, he was able to talk with his father about them, which he had been needing to do for a long time. Second, he also became aware that, because of his own experience, he had a special interest in providing support for cancer patients and their families. Now he could genuinely focus on *them* because of what he understood about himself. This self-knowledge freed him to care for others undergoing the struggle with cancer in a way he had not been able to do before. He had enriched his ability to care by taking advantage of his own rich, though painful, life experience, rather than avoiding it.

The second example focuses on Sally's encounter with a death situation. When the three-year-old child of her friends Cindy and Albert drowned in a lake near their home, Sally was sure that the couple would cling to each other for support. To her amazement, Cindy and Albert seemed to distance themselves with stony silences, interspersed with angry accusations. Cindy kept reminding Albert that she had never wanted to live with a small child close to a lake. Albert replied that if she hadn't been spending so much time talking with her friends on the telephone, she would have been a more responsible mother.

Sally was baffled by what was going on between Cindy and Albert. In her own family's experience, she remembered that during times of crisis, especially deaths, all of them had always pulled together. Why were Cindy and Albert not able to support each other in the same way? She found herself growing irritated with their "childish behavior." After pointing out their mistakes to them several times, Sally finally gave up in her attempts to patch things up between them. A year later Cindy and Albert were divorced.

Cindy and Albert's divorce had nothing to do with Sally's ability (or inability) to help. They were victims of a common reaction to the death of a child. The sense of grief and responsibility is so strong that people seek to avoid it by placing the blame on someone else. Sadly, the most available target is the other parent. Sally's only failure in seeking to care for Cindy and Albert lay in her expectation that they would respond to each other as her own family had done in times of loss. She was not aware of the dynamics at work in this particular kind of grief.

Sally and Tom both need to be more aware of the baggage brought to caring situations. This baggage that we bring includes past experiences, expectations placed on us by others, our own perceptions of how the world should be, and our natural personality characteristics. All of that adds up to a very heavy load.

Tom's baggage, in this particular case, consisted of unresolved grief over his mother's death. Failure to come to terms with that grief limited him in the care that he could extend to other grieving persons. The weight of that grief was unknown to him until he entered the cancer patient's room. Sally's baggage, on the other hand, was her limited knowledge on this particular issue. She assumed that because her own family had responded in one way, Cindy and Albert should respond similarly. She worked very hard at trying to show them the light. What worked for her family, Sally thought, must be workable for *all* families. Her baggage of assumptions carried from her own family background kept her from looking at Cindy and Albert's situation from another viewpoint. She did not know about the particular dynamics that affect a couple who have lost a child by death or the high incidence of divorce among couples who experience this tragedy.

Had Sally been aware of her need for additional information in order to broaden her self-knowledge, she could have been more sensitive to that particular situation. Tom's need was for expanded understanding of the experience that was already a part of him. All of us need both. As we become aware of this knowledge of self, we also become aware of our need for knowledge about human growth and development. The reflections at the end of this chapter will help you in becoming more aware of experiences of your own that may affect the caring relationship.

### Knowledge of Normal Human Development and Experiences in the Grief Process

The grief process is a basic example where knowledge about human development and experience will be helpful. Whether we are coping with death, divorce, aging, mid-life issues, or job loss, the common denominator is loss. As we develop an understanding of the grief process involved in all these loss experiences, we will also identify stages to help us choose more effective ways of caring.

When you become acquainted with some of the usual experiences through which people move, you may feel more comfortable staying with people in distress without becoming fearful that you are hurting rather than helping. There are also some danger signals you need to recognize. When you sense some of these danger points, it is time to consider making a referral, which we will discuss in the next chapter. But for now, our concern is to become familiar with the normal experience rather than with the abnormal.

## The Grief Process

Perhaps one of the most common experiences for all of us as human beings is that of loss. Throughout our lives we experience change and loss in our abilities, experiences, and relationships, and much of life is spent in a process of adjusting to these changes and losses.

Our reaction to loss is technically described as grief. Grief is the process within which one adjusts to the loss or absence of someone or something that has been highly valued. We can lose a relationship through death, divorce, unresolved conflict, or geographical moves such as job changes or going away to college. We may lose a sense of mastery and satisfaction because of job loss, aging, changing job requirements, or new working relationships. Children grow up and move away, creating a change in family interactions. The world changes, and we may have to leave behind dreams, hopes, values, and people in which we had invested ourselves.

So we are always in the process of coming to terms with losses. Many of them may seem minor because they are expected, but each of them carries a cost. All too often we deny the impact of a particular loss. Then, when a greater loss is suffered, we suddenly find ourselves facing grief over an accumulation of losses rather than just the most recent one. In one sense, it could be said that we are grieving all the time, because there is always some loss taking place in our lives.

Grief has been recorded in human history throughout the ages. Scripture presents us with pictures of its process in many places, but the Book of Job and the psalms of lament (such as Psalms 22 and 88) are focal points. The psalms of lament contain common elements of grief: intense and articulate description of the pain, memories of God's care in past times of loss, and confident praise of God for the promise of support in the present crisis.

Most modern studies have found that grieving progresses in a series of stages. These stages are not always neat and orderly, and a person may not move through them in a precise fashion. In fact, there is often a moving back and forth on the progressive scale. Nevertheless, there is a general process through which people typically move. Knowledge of these stages will serve not as a checklist but as an awareness of what is normal when people are describing their experiences.

Feelings can be intensely painful but at the same time be ultimately good. Therefore, do not make a well-meaning attempt to keep people from "feeling bad" when that is just what is needed in order for them to move on. Failure to move through the grief process after a significant loss can result in serious emotional or even physical difficulties in the future.

As you review the normal stages of the grief process, remember that people may vary as they move through these stages.

## Stage 1: Shock and Denial

When a loss occurs, the first stage of grief is shock and denial. We human beings don't like to lose things. And our "self" attempts to protect us from the pain of loss. In a self-protecting way, we try to save ourselves from knowing painful truth. That protection is seldom conscious and may occur in a variety of ways. Some people may faint upon hearing about the death of a loved one. Still others may appear to be hard of hearing. Their hearing may be fine under ordinary circumstances, but in a crisis the bad news must be told to them repeatedly in order for it to sink in. Hospital staff often have to pursue those who literally run away from bad news, believing that being in a different place will save them from the painful reality.

For most of us this period of shock and denial is a brief moment of feeling stunned—a moment of disbelief. The exclamation of "What?" or "I can't believe it!" is a typical initial response. We don't believe it because we don't want it to be true.

### Stage 2: Intermittent Waves

Following this first stage (usually very rapidly) comes a time of intermittent waves—a period of moving back and forth between the reality of the initial pain and a feeling of disbelief, or numbness. One analogy for this experience is that of standing in the surf at the beach. A wave comes in and knocks you off balance. Then there is a calm before the next wave comes in. So it goes with the feeling of being knocked off balance by the wave of pain, followed by a lull or sense of calm and relief before the next wave comes in. This second stage, like the first, is usually brief. Whereas the first stage usually lasts a matter of minutes or hours, this second stage may continue for a number of days.

### Stage 3: Acute Grief

Then comes the third stage, the acute period. During this time, we often wish for the relief of stages 1 and 2. Now the pain is usually acute and prolonged. Even when it is somewhat dulled, there is a feeling of fatigue and a sense that time is moving very slowly. Our first association with acute pain is crying. And that is certainly the way many people respond to the pain of grief. But other feelings can be healthy expressions of grief as well.

Some people express their sense of loss through anger. Others retreat into silence and give little external evidence of their pain. If your typical expression of hurt is through tears, it may surprise you to see other people reacting with anger or silence. But it is important to remember that each of these forms can be the same in terms of basic hurt. Just as some of us respond to stress with headaches and others with upset stomachs, so there are a variety of ways in which grief is manifested.

The one characteristic that is shared by all these responses to loss in the acute period is the degree of emotional intensity. Suffering has been described as the overwhelming wish that things were other than they are. The intensity of that pain is the most important thing for you to recognize when caring for someone in this stage of grief. Let the words of the psalmist instruct you as you seek to understand the power of this acute pain:

My God, my God, why hast thou forsaken me?
  Why art thou so far from helping me, from the
    words of my groaning?
O my God, I cry by day, but thou dost not answer;
  and by night, but find no rest. (Psalm 22:1–2)

The tone of voice in which these words are expressed can reveal either anger or despair. Each reading is a valid expression of the sense of pain experienced by the individual. The pain's acuteness is the most important characteristic of this third stage. Because you may be uncomfortable in the presence of another's pain, you may be tempted at this point to give up listening and try to "fix it" so the person won't hurt anymore.

Remember, the purpose of your listening is to enable people to move through their own individual grief process. It is their grief, not yours, and they need to express it in their own way and on their own time schedule. So when you are caring for someone, you may find yourself responding in one of three ways:

1. Running away from them and their pain
2. Blocking their path or setting up stumbling blocks
3. Walking *with* them, enabling their pilgrimage through the grief process

The first two responses may express your natural instincts, but the third is a more disciplined and caring response to a person in acute grief.

### Stage 4: Remembering

Following the period of acute grief comes a longer and less intense, but nonetheless important, fourth stage of grief—remembering. During the first three stages, loss is experienced as something external. It is as if the threat is "out there" and needs to be fought, if not conquered. In order for us to come to some resolution of the pain, the loss must eventually be internalized and accepted as a part of us. It needs to be taken in and made a part of our life experience rather than remaining an enemy that invades our sense of stability at unpredictable moments. Remembering is a psychological ritual that enables us to incorporate loss slowly and place it in its proper perspective.

A beautiful example of this stage of remembering as a means of bringing about resolution took place in a parish that was struck by a tornado several years ago. Following the destruction caused by the storm, many members and neighbors gathered at the church. For the first several hours, the first three stages of grief were obvious. People looked dazed and overwhelmed. "I can't believe it," was the recurring statement. Then too, there were tears and periods of anger and frustration as people moved through the next two stages. For two weeks people continued to gather at the church for meals, first aid, rest room facilities, and use of a telephone.

During those two weeks a significant thing took place. People began to tell stories. Meal after meal, at table after table, people told each other what had happened to them just before, during, and after the storm. What no one recognized consciously was the importance of this remembering and the reliving of the events over and over again. As those stories were told, healing was taking place. As individuals shared their fears and anxieties, common solutions began to emerge. No longer did they feel alone in their struggle. The power of private fears was broken by sharing in community. What had been intensely threatening became shared remembrances—stories to be told. The storm was not forgotten, but it no longer had the power to control their lives.

In contrast, the people who did not sit around those tables or engage in any other process of working through the experience remained victims of the storm. A year later, whenever the wind would pick up, those persons would find themselves experiencing various degrees of fear and hysteria. They would run to their basements, cry, become angry, or consider moving away. Bad weather was still an enemy unconquered.

Many people believe that to stop thinking about something or someone is a way of maintaining control. The fact is, the harder we try to bury things inside us, the more powerful they become. Even though we think we have things under control, thoughts pop up at unexpected and inappropriate times and *take* control of us. When we choose to remember actively instead of trying to forget or avoid, there are a number of benefits that can be realized. Here are three:

1. Verbalizing our memories weakens the power of grief over us by exposing it. Pent-up feelings tend to be overwhelming and debilitating, somewhat like nightmares. Exposing our grief to the light of day enables us to see more clearly what we must face, just as turning on the light dispels darkness and the bad dream.

2. Remembering enables us to put loss in the past rather than allowing it to stay alive, controlling the present. Major loss cannot be completely forgotten (nor should it be), but that loss needs to be put in proper perspective. For example, when the loss is the death of a loved one, keeping the memory alive cannot bring back the person, but memory does preserve the richness that the relationship brought to one's life.

3. Sharing our memories with another person allows grief to become the responsibility of a caring community rather than leaving it as a lonely, individual burden. Shared feelings tend to ease the tension and connect us with other people who will share the pain with us rather than leaving us alone.

Frank, whom you met in the first two chapters, was not able to extend himself to Mary because he had not yet experienced for himself the benefit of remembering. Mary's pain triggered emotion in him that was not yet resolved. Therefore he avoided her pain, thinking it was best for her.

As you can see, this stage of remembering is very significant. In fact, some of the most important recovery that takes place does so during this stage, which may last for an extended period of time. Unfortunately, many people are not aware that some of the best ministry to persons in grief occurs months after the loss. We live in a world that gives people a few days off after a death and then expects things to get back to normal. Yet, as the weeks go by, the impact of a major loss begins to take its toll in the midst of an environment that discourages us from talking about painful issues. So the benefits of remembering, discussed earlier, often go unrealized.

Therefore some of the most effective caring that you can do during the stage of remembering is to make contact with a person who has suffered a loss. Special times of the year, such as birthdays, anniversaries, and holidays, are particularly difficult for the grieving person. A letter, a telephone call, or a visit shows that you remember too. When talking with the person, don't find everything else to talk about *except* the loss. Go ahead and say, "I called you because I know that this is the first Christmas without Ruth, and I wanted you to know I was thinking about you." You may find yourself greeted by a flood of memories from the grieving person. And if you can remain with the person, can listen with an understanding nod, and let the memories come, you will have given a very precious gift.

## Stage 5: Acceptance—Reinvestment

Many writers describe the final stage of grief as one of acceptance. The term implies that resolution has taken place and that the grieving person is ready to move on with life. It is very important to keep in mind that acceptance does not imply forgetting. The term "reinvestment" may clarify the meaning of acceptance. Whatever or whoever has been lost is not replaced, but the survivor begins to find other activities and people to meet some of the needs that were formerly met by the person or thing that was lost.

Acceptance, or reinvestment, is the point at which the loss has been taken in and made a part of the self. For example, after the death of his wife, a man eventually is able to say, "I am a widower." The loss now is an identifiable part of who he is, and that loss can be discussed without his feeling overwhelmed by the pain. In addition, that loss can now be viewed as a new reservoir of understanding that can be extended to others experiencing a similar loss. Rather than avoiding other people's pain, because it triggers too much discomfort, he may even seek out opportunities to care for others in the early stages of their own loss.

An excellent example of ways in which people can carry through with reinvestment is found in recovery groups. CanSurmount, for example, brings together people who have experienced the sufferings and losses of cancer in themselves or in loved ones. They support each other and extend themselves to others who are facing similar circumstances. Tom, in our earlier example, might have benefited from such a group. You can gain information about such support groups in your area by calling the American Cancer Society.

The Compassionate Friends serves a similar purpose for families who have suffered the death of a child. In most areas this organization is listed in the telephone directory. Cindy and Albert, in our second example, might have gained insight into their loss and gained support through such sharing in this kind of recovery group.

The grief process is a fundamental human experience that we need to understand, not only for our own well-being but in order to care effectively. Although much of our attention has focused on the experience of death, we face many other losses in our lives. Divorce, job loss, aging, career changes, midlife transitions, and geographical moves all involve giving up something in which we have invested. Even if the giving up is something we choose, loss is still suffered. That is a surprise to some people, who find themselves troubled by grief when they should be happy. Once again, if we understand what is going on, we have an opportunity to share our caring.

## Warning: This May Be Hazardous to Your Caring

Knowledge of these stages is valuable for your understanding and insight. It provides you with a guideline for evaluating normal human experience. However, guidelines may be dangerous if you use them to push people to "act normal" or to decide for them in which stage they should be. Our hope is that your awareness of these stages will enable you to be a companion with persons in grief rather than tempt you to set yourself up as a detached instructor, directing them from a distance. *Never, never,* fall into the trap of telling someone, "Well, you are clearly in Stage Three. Don't you think it is time to move on?" Your responses to persons in grief need to show that you are listening compassionately and are with them no matter what stage they are presently going through. Your *knowing* the stages enables you to stay with them during this time instead of trying to put them somewhere else. Your *listening* enables them to move through their grief process at their own rate.

## For Your Reflection

One of the most helpful ways to master an understanding of the grief process is to identify its stages in your own life. So give yourself some time to reflect. This is not something that can be done in a hurry. Take pencil and paper and begin to record your own memories of a significant loss in your life. Don't worry at first about finding stages. Just write down the memories.

After you have written as much as seems appropriate, look back over your notes and see whether the stages seem to be identifiable. Remember that the stages don't move along neatly in order, and you may even find that you moved back and forth between them. Perhaps a stage seems to be entirely missing. You may find that, while you thought you had completed your grief, you haven't. What still needs to take place? Is there someone with whom you need to do some remembering?

While the process may be painful at points, we believe that you will also find some things to celebrate. Being able to verbalize some of the specific gifts left to you by that person has a special kind of richness.

After going over your grief process, try talking with a good friend or close family member about your own experience or one of theirs. This will sensitize you in a way that will enrich your caring for others.

## For Your Devotional Thought

Read Psalms 46, 61, and 130. Note the articulate despair of the writers. Note the desire for and experience of hope by the writer of Psalm 130. These writers know the power of grief, and, more important, they know of God's power and presence in their lives, sharing their pain and loss.

Now add to your knowledge gained from the psalms the power of this passage from 2 Corinthians 1:3–4. "Blessed be the God and Father of our Lord Jesus Christ, the Father of mercies and God of all comfort, who comforts us in all our affliction, so that we may be able to comfort those who are in any affliction, with the comfort with which we ourselves are comforted by God."

It is good to give thanks for God's presence in our lives during times of grief. In response to this gracious gift, we have the opportunity to be present with others in ways that are faithful to God's love.

*Gracious God, thank you for the grace that comes to us in all times and places. Thank you for the gift of your child, whom you were willing to sacrifice so that we might know the magnitude of your love. Thank you for enabling us to extend that love to others through our caring. Amen.*

# 6

# Warning Signals
# and Referral

This chapter introduces you to particular crises and situations that call for intensive and specific skills—skills that have been developed through extensive and specialized training. In your caring for others it is very important to know when to call in professionals.

Perhaps it would be well to draw a distinction here between care and counseling. Care, as we have defined it in this book, involves a relationship of relative equality. When you visit a person grieving the death of a loved one, you go in the knowledge that you could easily be in that same position. You can't "fix" the person's pain, nor will you be expected to. You go as a fellow pilgrim through life, willing to extend a hand as you walk that path together. The care you extend is in the form of a very general but limited invitation. As you invite, you do so as a caregiver, not as a counselor.

Counseling, on the other hand, is a relationship in which one party has relatively more authority because of extensive, formal training in therapy. There is a mutual acknowledgment between the counselor and the one or more counselees that there is a specific, relatively serious problem that calls for attention. The parties agree from the beginning to schedule regular times to work on the issues in a carefully structured environment.

A second agreement is that the counselee gives permission to the counselor to probe into specific personal matters. This process is much more intense and personal than what we have defined in this book as a caring relationship.

A third area of agreement is that the counselor has specific knowledge and, at points, prescriptions to be offered to the counselee as a way of coping with the difficulties. Such giving of advice is not ordinarily a part of a more general caring relationship. In fact, it should be avoided.

Once this distinction between general caring and specific counseling is drawn, a question remains. How is the caregiver to know when more specific counseling and intervention is needed? Some warning signals will be described in this chapter. There will also be a description of some of the different professions that are available to provide support when situations arise that are more than you are prepared to handle. And some of the steps you can take in making a referral that is supportive to the troubled person will be outlined.

## Warning Signals

First, in trying to detect serious difficulty in a person's functioning, simply watch for changes in normal, everyday behavior. These warning signals usually can be spotted very easily. The most common things we do in life revolve around eating, sleeping, work, relationships, and use of leisure time, and we develop habits in all these areas. In fact, we human beings tend to be very predictable creatures over time. Therefore, when you notice a change taking place in these ordinary activities of someone, you need to ask yourself whether the change is the result of some *conscious* decision the person has made to alter the rhythm of his or her living or whether the change is a reflection of some disturbance to the normal routine.

## Eating

In the realm of eating, when one is upset one tends to start eating either more or less. The more or less isn't the issue. The *change* is. So if someone is gaining weight or losing it, it might be well to try to discover what it means. In our present-day preoccupation with fitness, weight loss may mean that someone is dieting. But it may also mean that person is worrying or is under stress and hasn't even noticed that she or he is eating less and losing weight. The only chance you have to find out what is going on is to comment on the change and wonder about it out loud. That gives the person an opportunity to explain or take you up on your invitation to talk about it.

In the same way, a person may be eating more without even being aware of it, and the pounds are piling on. Even if such persons are conscious of it, they can't seem to make themselves stop eating.

One way of noticing these changes is found in the case of Joan. After taking an early retirement, Joan decided that she would do some things for herself that she had neglected for a long time. She began to exercise and lose weight.

There were three different kinds of reactions to her visible weight loss:

1. "Joan! You have lost so much weight. You look really great."

2. "Hi, Joan. How are you doing?" (The person obviously notices the change in weight but says nothing.)

3. "Joan, I've noticed you've been losing weight. I hope it's on purpose."

Responses 1 and 2 are polite, but they don't offer Joan an opportunity for help if she wants it. The only acceptable reply to the first response is a polite "Thank you." Replying to what the person in the second response has noticed would take a lot of gumption.

Response 3, however, gives Joan the option to say, "Yes, I've been dieting, and it's worked. Thanks for noticing." Or, if she is in distress, she could say, "Well, a lot of things have been bothering me lately. Have you got a few minutes?"

The emphasis here, as throughout the book, is on giving an invitation that is open-ended. In this particular case, Joan is not likely to ask for help. But if she is feeling a sense of loss because of her retirement, at least the third response gives her an opportunity to say so.

To refer back to our discussion of grief, it is not at all unusual to see a person change eating patterns in the days and weeks following a loss. But if that change continues for months and even years, we have a warning signal of potential difficulty.

### Sleeping

Just as some people may change their eating patterns when adversity strikes, others experience sleep disturbances. Difficulty in getting to sleep, waking up earlier than usual, or fitful tossing all through the night—any of these may be a warning signal that something is wrong. Sure, one sleep-disturbed night may just be the result of something eaten earlier that day, but what about the disturbance that goes on night after night? Then you have a signal that more than a poor choice of food or drink is involved. When you hear a person talking about extended periods of difficulty in sleeping, it is time again to wonder out loud about what is going on.

If you are aware that there has been a major loss, or the first child is going off to college, or the business is in trouble, then the person doesn't necessarily have major emotional difficulties that call for referral. But you *do* now recognize an opportunity for caring and can be confident in extending an invitation. However, if the disturbance has been going on for an inordinate period of time and there seems to be little awareness of the causes, you need to consider making a referral.

## Work

We all have our own patterns of work with a regular level of productivity. The pattern varies from one person to the next, but we all have a sense of when we are working normally. There are times when someone may experience a surge of creativity or times when one just can't seem to concentrate. The reasons may be readily explainable, but if the lower energy level or nonproductivity continues over a long period of time, you may begin to wonder about what is going on in that person's life. Wondering out loud extends an invitation for caring. On the one hand, it is no more than a comment that indicates you have noticed. On the other hand, your noticing says a great deal about your caring.

## Relationships

The process of living with special people in our lives never remains static, but there are still reasonably predictable patterns. When you see those patterns begin to change in people, it is time to wonder again. Do they seem to be getting along better? Maybe you would do well to comment on it and celebrate with them in their newfound richness. Do they seem to be getting more irritable, or are they avoiding each other? Maybe you need to notice that they seem more upset and then invite them to tell you about it.

Their answer may be that the children have gotten

into trouble, causing a great deal of stress within the family. Or the answer may be that their marriage is in real trouble and may be coming apart. What can they do? That's when your noticing has paid off. But what if you have found out more than you feel ready to handle? Your caring has opened a door, but you feel that you can't walk through it with them. Then they need another kind of helper. This is the time for referral.

### Leisure Time

Some people may just never make time for leisure. If that is their pattern, then that's OK. We're not going to tell anyone how to work or how to relax. We aren't making a judgment on the patterns themselves. We're just looking for *changes* in patterns already established. If a workaholic woman suddenly starts staying home, you need to check on whether she was fired, or whether she has realized the need for some rest. When the regular tennis player reports that he has just been too tired to play, you might comment on that being a real change for him. Then, as with all invitations, you wait to see what comes next, willing to continue to listen and care. If the degree of disturbance seems inconsistent with the reasons given, it is time to begin wondering more seriously about making a referral.

### Evaluating What You Notice

When a person reports a disturbance in any *one* of these areas of eating, sleeping, working, relating, or relaxing, you are right to be concerned, but you can also be relatively certain that the disturbance is one that you can address. However, if you find disturbances in *several* of these areas, you need to begin thinking seriously about making a referral.

In other words, a single disturbance is probably not

a sufficient basis to warrant probing for more serious difficulty. There are several variables to consider: length of time, intensity, and level of awareness.

## Length of Time

Remember that in discussing the grief process we pointed out various lengths of normal time for each stage. Shock and denial, for instance, ordinarily last only hours or, at the most, days. Intermittent waves last a bit longer, as does the intense period. Remembering may linger the most. Therefore, in evaluating the propriety of a person's stage of grief, the length of time is an important variable. If a person reports, "My husband died three years ago, and I have never cried," the length of time is inappropriate, and a more serious difficulty may well be in process. Or a person who lost an infant ten years ago may still become upset whenever she hears a baby cry. Again, the length of time since the death tells you that this expression of the third stage of grief just doesn't fit the normal pattern.

## Intensity

As with length of time, the intensity of emotion expressed by a person needs to be evaluated in relation to the loss or stress that is being faced. If a woman bursts into sobs when telling you about the death of Aunt Sarah's dog, you should begin to wonder what is really being grieved. It may well be that this particular incident unblocked an old grief she had not been able to express. Your noticing that her emotion is more intense than you would have expected could open the way to some serious working through of her grief or even move her into professional counseling to deal with her old wounds.

## Level of Awareness

Last but not least, watch for the degree of con-
sciousness about the situation that a person seems to
have when talking about important issues or when
exhibiting intense emotion. If the person sobbing
over the death of a relatively unknown pet does not
seem aware that such sobbing is inappropriate in the
circumstances, that is something to worry about. On
the other hand, if the person says, "You know, I'm
surprised at how upset I have been since hearing that
news. It doesn't make sense, since I never even knew
her dog," then you have a situation that is not as
serious. She is already aware that something else is
going on and is more likely to do something about it.
Later, if necessary, the door is open for you to both
listen and provide direction in suggesting more help
for her.

## A Case for Your Evaluation

Beverly is a faithful member of your congregation.
You don't know her very well personally, but you are
accustomed to seeing her in various leadership posi-
tions in the church. As a member of the pastoral care
committee of your church, you are asked to visit Beverly, who has just returned home after a brief stay in
the hospital. It seems that she became dehydrated
during a bout with the flu and was briefly hospital-
ized to receive additional fluids.

After calling in advance to set a time for your
visit, you arrive at her home and she greets you
warmly at the door. After a bit of idle chitchat,
you, the visitor, say:

VISITOR: Beverly, I'm glad to have a chance to
visit with you. My main purpose in
coming today is to see how you are
doing after your recent illness and what
we in the church can do to be helpful.

But I'm also glad just to get to know you better.

*(Beverly nods graciously, and suddenly you see tears in her eyes.)*

VISITOR *(leaning forward, having been trained well by Arnold and Fohl):* Beverly, are you OK?

BEVERLY: Sure. I'm fine. What makes you ask?

VISITOR: Well, I noticed you had tears in your eyes, and I wanted you to know that I care about whatever you're going through.

BEVERLY: Thanks. It's true that this flu has really worn me out. I'm aware of feeling very tired, and I notice I've even been getting teary at times. I guess I've been pushing myself so hard that it took the flu to slow me down. What I need to do is take better stock of myself and start recognizing some of my limits.

VISITOR: You sound like you need to look more closely at how you use your time and how you manage your energy.

BEVERLY: Yes, I do. And it really helps to do a little thinking out loud with someone. Thanks for being here. Can you stay a little longer?

Don't you wish it would always turn out this way? Well, sometimes it does, and you would continue to nurture the relationship that has already begun here. But it is also possible that the visit could have gone like this:

VISITOR: Beverly, I'm glad to have a chance to visit with you. My main purpose in coming today is to see how you are after your recent illness, and what we in the church can do to be helpful. But I'm also glad just to get to know you better.

*(Beverly nods graciously, and suddenly you see tears in her eyes.)*

VISITOR     *(leaning forward):* Beverly, are you OK?

BEVERLY:  Oh, sure. I'm fine. What makes you ask?

VISITOR:   Well, I noticed you had tears in your eyes, and I wanted you to know that I care about whatever you're going through.

BEVERLY:  Thanks, but there's no way you can help. *(Pause.)*

*(Visitor listens but doesn't say anything.)*

BEVERLY:  Everything is falling apart. I work hard at the church, and what good does it do me? My husband and I fight constantly, I'm so tired I can't get sleep, and my doctor keeps telling me to stop losing weight. I guess I just want to waste away to nothing, because that's the way I feel—like a nothing.

Now what? This is just exactly what can happen in making a visit. All of a sudden a barrage of feeling comes out. Beverly's brief, relatively minor medical treatment has opened the floodgates for a great deal of intense emotion. Our visitor may stay and listen for a while, but it is evident here that much more is going on than a normal recovery from hospitalization. You need to recognize the warning signals that are present in this second scenario. The question now is, What do you do when those warning signals *do* appear so clearly? How do you make a helpful referral?


**Resources Available to You**

One of the nice things about being involved in caring is the discovery of the number of other people out there who are ready and willing to back you up.

There is real truth in the maxim that you are never alone. There are literally dozens, if not hundreds, of professional people of various sorts who are trained and available to provide support to persons in need of special attention during times of difficulty. Counseling, however, is an inexact science. You won't find absolute agreement from one professional to the next as to the preferable form of treatment or even on the diagnosis of what is wrong. Nonetheless, there are specialists among the mental health professionals who can assist you in making an appropriate referral. In the few pages that follow is a very brief description of some of the most important helping professionals available in most communities.

## Pastors

Let's begin with your own pastor. We have assumed that your caring is being done in some way within the context of your faith community. You may or may not be involved in an organized caring program of your church, but in any case your pastor should be someone who has had at least some degree of basic orientation to care and counseling. While not ordinarily a trained therapist, a parish pastor usually has two very basic things to offer.

First, parish pastors should have some developed listening skills that will help them to assess generally what is going on with a troubled person. The listening skills, in combination with the authority role of the minister, often can help to bring stability to a situation while more specialized help is being explored.

Second, parish pastors ordinarily have already spent some time getting to know mental health professionals, attorneys, and physicians in the community. In other words, your pastor is often one of the best resources for referral that you can find. Mention the problems you have run into, and you will probably discover that some good resources are available.

## A Comment on Confidentiality

No sooner do we say something about telling the pastor what you have stumbled into than the question rightly arises: What if the person hasn't given permission for me to tell the pastor? To ask that question is to raise the issue of confidentiality.

Confidentiality, to many people, simply means keeping a secret. That is unfortunate, since keeping secrets often results in more harm than helpfulness. The aim of confidentiality is to protect people from harm by controlling the circulation of information. A great deal of hurt can be caused by untrained persons trying to handle sensitive information about others, especially when this turns into simple gossip.

Confidentiality, then, doesn't mean "not telling anybody anything." Rather, it means that you will be very selective about whom you will tell. Therefore, while the best policy is to get prior permission to discuss a situation with the pastor or any other professional, there are times when it may be necessary to share "secrets" in order to protect the person from harm. To do so is a judgment call that is sometimes very difficult. We hope you will develop confidence and trust in some professional, perhaps your pastor, that enables you to share confidentialities. And we hope you will know that you are doing so in order to *help* or *get help,* not just to tell secrets.

## Pastoral Counselors

Pastoral counselors are ministers who combine the comfort of pastoral care and the skill of specialized counseling in difficult emotional and relational situations. Depression, prolonged grief, marital and family difficulties, and adjustment to stress are some of the situations for which pastoral counselors are trained to help. Again, your pastor probably has knowledge of a pastoral counseling center in your area. And your telephone directory may have a listing. While some churches provide free pastoral counseling services, more often a fee (usually on a sliding scale) is charged.

## Physicians

Medical doctors who specialize in general medicine or family practice are often excellent resources for persons in trouble. While we immediately associate them with treatment for physical problems, often the bodily complaints are an outgrowth of deeper emotional difficulties. If the doctor has already seen the person about whom you are concerned, the suggestion that the person call the doctor may be the best option. Or you may want to call the physician and report your concern. An advantage here is that the doctor should have helpful suggestions if more specialized help is needed.

## Psychiatrists

In addition to having a medical degree, psychiatrists also have extensive training in counseling. They are able to respond to both physical and emotional problems. When emotional support needs further assistance through medication, these are the professionals to whom you should turn.

## Social Workers

Social workers are the people to contact if you need to know facts about eligibility for help in obtaining food, fuel, housing, clothing, welfare benefits, Social Security, rehabilitation services, and many other basic necessities. They can be found both in commu-

nity agencies and in private practice. Many are also
trained in counseling. They are excellent resources
in a crisis situation, as well as a bountiful source of
information about your community.

### Community Mental Health Services

Most communities have mental health services
with a variety of specialists whose primary concern
is providing resources for emotional and mental well-
being. Psychologists, psychiatrists, social workers,
pastoral counselors, specialized nurses—all these and
more are available. Ordinarily there is someone on
call around the clock to accept telephone calls and
provide counsel about how to handle a difficult or
crisis situation. These specialists will provide support
for you as you seek help for a troubled person and can
guide you in deciding whether a referral is necessary.
Your local newspaper or telephone directory lists
numbers for hot lines and specialized crisis intervention services that are frequently supported by these
mental health centers.

### Private Practice Counselors

There are more kinds of counselors than we could
list here. Many are very good. Many are very bad. We
would not advise simply picking one out of the telephone directory. Your pastor and your family physician are usually the best professionals from whom to
gain information about the competent counselors in
your community. Counselors, of course, do charge a
fee for their services, but in many instances these
fees are reimbursable by medical insurance.

### Referrals: The Art of Getting Help

Two of the most significant dimensions of getting
help have already been discussed in earlier parts of

this chapter. First, be aware of the warning signals that more professional help may be needed. The description of the grief process in chapter 5 helps you to recognize the normality of intense emotion. We are all human beings with feelings. When we lose something that matters, we are going to be upset. But when that grief (or some other emotion) takes too much control over us for too long, then it is time to get more professional help. Knowing the warning signals described in this chapter should both give you courage and make you cautious.

Take courage in the fact that you now know some things to watch out for. But, at the same time, be cautious. Acknowledge your limits. Don't try to "fix" something yourself when you see that there may be a more serious disturbance going on than you have been trained to handle. Getting help is not an admission of defeat. It is an act of good common sense, which in this case involves an understanding of yourself and your limits.

The second dimension discussed in this chapter involved knowing the resources available to you. Be willing to acknowledge the expertise of individuals and call on the people and institutions you know that are equipped to handle more difficult situations. Bear in mind that, apart from pastors, professional persons are not free to initiate contact. Once you have obtained the name of several willing professionals, it may become your task to encourage the troubled person to call one of them for an appointment.

### Checking It Out

Recognizing another person's need for help and knowing the resources available are activities that largely take place in your head. Now comes the delicate part. What do you *do?* First, check out your impressions with another trusted person *in confidence.* Two possibilities exist here. The first one is more desirable. Talk over the situation with the person who you think needs help. You may very well be close enough simply to say, "Jonathan, I have been worrying about you. You just don't seem to be getting back to your old self after all these months. Do you think you might need some help?" That sort of query invites Jonathan to be a partner with you in evaluating and making a decision about whether further help is needed. Often, just mentioning your concern can be the impetus in moving him to seek additional help. Your invitation may enable him to acknowledge actively his unnamed demon and stir him to action.

If you do not sense that you can ask the person directly (and you have to trust your instincts in making that decision), you need to discuss the situation with someone experienced in disciplined caring. It may not be appropriate for you to call a professional person yourself in order to make the referral. But your pastor and your own family physician are excellent resources to call on in order to describe your concerns and solicit advice.

### Making the Suggestion

Next, if the decision for referral is indicated, determine who should make the suggestion. If you have already checked it out with the person, it is an easy transition. "Jonathan, I'm glad you agree that something more is needed. Perhaps you already have a doctor, but, if not, I think Dr. Cecil is an excellent resource. He is a very caring person who has worked with many other people over the years who were struggling with depression, and his office is not far from where you work." Notice that the suggestion is accompanied with some specific information about the resource. The more you know about the resource person, the more confidence you inspire in the person needing the help. Again, this is the reason it is so important for you to know about the resources available in your community.

However, sometimes you feel that you are not the best person to make the suggestion that further help seems needed. In this case, contact a pastor or a physician, who, in turn, takes the initiative in suggesting help. The pastor or the physician might mention your caring by saying, "Jonathan, I'm here because Mary has expressed concern about your difficulty in getting out very much lately. We both have worried about you and wondered whether you need some help. Could we talk a bit?" You can justifiably experience a sense of pride and relief in identifying a need, exploring it carefully, and initiating the next level of continued care.

## *Following Through*

Once a person goes for further help, don't just forget about it. Professionals have their limitations too. Counselors, for instance, ordinarily see someone on a weekly basis and deal with very intense and focused issues. People need that kind of specific help, but they also need more. Continue to drop by or call on the telephone. Don't make specific inquiries about what is being discussed with the counselor; that is confidential. But *do* communicate continuing interest and willingness to spend time with the person. After all, your caring is still there, although the responsibility is being shared among a number of people.

## For Your Reflection

Take a few moments to look through the yellow pages of your local telephone directory in order to learn what resources are available in your own community. Look under counseling, counselors, psychologists, mental health services, psychiatrists (usually listed under physicians), and similar headings. Ask your pastor, or a friend who is a professional counselor, to suggest names of trusted resources. Make a list of persons that you will have on hand in order to make an appropriate referral.

### For Your Devotional Thought

Read Ephesians 4:11–16. After doing so, think again about the gifts that are yours to offer to other people. Then think about the gifts you do not have. Although you may first be tempted to be envious of those gifts, take time to allow yourself to experience gratitude for the gifts you do not have that have been shared with you by others. This is part of the genius about the way in which God created us. Because we are limited creatures, we must be in relationship with others in order to receive. If we can move past the wish that we "had it all," we can experience the richness of what it means to share out of gratitude with one another.

Now take your meditation one step farther. When we work together in community, the gifts of others are often ours to share. When you perceive a need in another person that you cannot fulfill, the gift that you do have is the knowledge of someone who may fill that need. To engage in the sharing of each other's gifts (such as making a good referral) is one of the most powerful expressions of what it means for us to be a priesthood of believers.

*Gracious and all-wise God, thank you for not equipping me to deal with everything. Thank you for putting me in community, where others are able to fill those gaps where I am lacking. Thank you for giving me relationships within which I can both work and experience the fullness of your love. Grant me the wisdom to see both my gifts and my limits. Cultivate in me a willingness to be one of a priesthood of those who care. Amen.*

# 7

# Sharing
# in Everyday Life

Mrs. Warner, a special education resource teacher, was leaving her schoolroom after class and noticed Katie, a fourth-grade student, standing in the hall outside the library, her head low. That was unusual behavior for this particularly vivacious ten-year-old child. Now what?

If you were Mrs. Warner, how could you show that you care? Or should you? What are some of the options that occur to you after having come this far in thinking about sharing our caring?

Some possible responses are:

1. Keep on walking. After all, you don't want to be nosy, and students don't want to talk to a teacher anyway.
2. Say "Hi" to Katie and keep on walking.
3. Keep what you have seen in mind for future reference if and when this behavior is repeated.
4. Talk with Katie's teacher about how Katie is doing in her class.
5. Call Katie's parents and tell them you were wondering why Katie is looking so sad recently.
6. Stop and ask Katie why she looks so sad.
7. Stop and talk to Katie for a while. Don't ask specifically about her feelings. Just give her a chance to visit with you for a few minutes.

This list may give you more alternatives than you would ever want to consider. But you can see the dilemma. Daily we observe people and wonder whether they need something or whether it would even be appropriate for us to offer our help. All too often the decision seems too much for us. Consequently we choose to do nothing. We excuse ourselves by remembering that, as children, we were taught to be polite and not to "stick our noses into other people's business."

Of course, it is also true that there *are* times when it would be inappropriate to invade another person's life by asking personal questions. That is the reason so much emphasis was placed in chapter 3 on the importance of initiating our caring in the form of an invitation. The list of alternatives that we have suggested for Mrs. Warner covers the gamut from noninvolvement to an invitation that is respectful but noninvasive. All of them are alternatives in caregiving. There is no one right answer.

Alternative 1 is a decision not to get involved, and there may be very good reasons for it. Mrs. Warner may be completely drained that day and not able to extend herself further. Or perhaps she thinks it is not a good idea to get involved with a student just then when it is a time that they both should be in class. Or there may be other circumstances that are just as valid.

Alternative 2 is the "be polite" decision, an important option and one that all of us should know. Smiling at Katie at least acknowledges a level of relationship between teacher and student.

Alternative 3 is also an important option. As caregivers, we store information about people we know. When we see a certain pattern developing, we can use this information later in our invitation to care for them.

Alternatives 4 and 5 are referral options. We see

something and are unsure of the best way to deal with it. So we consult with someone who may know more about the situation or be able to do something more constructive for the person.

Alternatives 6 and 7 are the most involving. Alternative 6 is more invasive. In a real sense, Mrs. Warner pushes into Katie's world with an assumption that something is wrong. Alternative 7, if done well, represents an attempt to carry out the form of invitation in caring that is described in this book.

You may well be wondering why in the world you need to sort all this out when you see a little girl standing in the hallway looking a bit downcast. And one answer is that it really isn't that big a deal. If no one initiates some caring for Katie on this particular occasion, she probably will still survive and get along very well. On the other hand, all of us are carrying around a number of losses or hurts in our lives all the time. When the moment comes when someone invites us to unburden ourselves, it is a very special time. And that is exactly what happened in this incident involving Mrs. Warner and Katie.

Mrs. Warner chose alternative 6. She stopped, looked at Katie, and said, "Katie, are you OK?"

KATIE *(looking up with tears in her eyes, but forcing a smile):* Yes, ma'am. I'm fine.

Another crossroads. Mrs. Warner could have decided at this point that she had done her duty and proceeded on down the hall. Obviously Katie wanted her to think that everything was all right. Again, as before, a number of alternatives are possible here. You can probably list them for yourself, but we will continue with the story.

MRS. WARNER: Well, you don't *look* like everything is OK. Can I help?

KATIE *(who, at this point, has a number of alternatives herself!):* Well . . .

*(Long pause, while Mrs. Warner waits patiently.)* It's really kind of dumb.

MRS. WARNER *(stooping down to be on her level):* Try me. I'd like to hear about it.

KATIE *(looking at Mrs. Warner for the first time, although sheepishly):* Well, I've got three books that are overdue, and . . . well . . . the librarian told me that if I didn't bring them in by today that she'd have to call my mom, and . . . well, I sort of lied to her and told her that we'd lost them, because I didn't want her to call home. But now she says she has to call my mom anyway and tell her how much the books cost. *(Starts getting teary.)*

MRS. WARNER: Oh, Katie, that must make you feel bad, but I'm sure your mother will understand. All of us lose things.

KATIE: Well *(bowing her head again)*, it's just that I don't want to bother her now. *(Pause.)* She has so much to worry about right now.

Crossroads again!

Now what? Does Mrs. Warner continue to invite Katie to unload about what is going on at home? Here is the good caregiver, already late for her next class. She has tried to be helpful, never suspecting what she might encounter. Now she has really opened a can of worms. No wonder people are apt to choose one of our first three alternatives. One of the risks of genuine caring is that you may find yourself in a situation that is more involving than you had anticipated.

It is in these everyday encounters in life that we may find the greatest opportunities for caring. Certain crisis points, such as death, demand our attention. But the day-in-and-day-out conversations often provide another significant arena for extending our care to others. Hurt is not confined to the dramatic events of life. Often there are painful, silent situations that breed discomfort or even despair. These hurts do not cry out as do death or divorce or physical pain, but the hurt is just as real.

This is especially true for children who have neither ways to communicate their hurt nor ways to handle it. It is obvious from this encounter with Mrs. Warner that Katie is upset about more than library books. The librarian may have missed this, but Mrs. Warner, by extending herself at a crucial time, has an opportunity to care in a deeper way.

What is Mrs. Warner to do? As outlined in chapter 3, three dimensions are involved in initiating a relationship. Mrs. Warner has already (1) *extended an invitation,* (2) *defined* herself as more than a teacher, and now (3) has suddenly found herself in the position of *gathering more information* than she had expected. It is that additional information which now makes her uncertain about where or how to proceed.

Mrs. Warner, having committed herself this far in the conversation, now has two realistic alternatives. One is to continue to talk with Katie herself to find out what the situation is and deal with the problem herself. Or she can use the resources available in the school (Katie's teacher and the school counselor) in order to *share* the caring for Katie. As indicated in chapter 6, there are a variety of people to help when we feel limited. Mrs. Warner feels that way now. She is limited by time and by lack of information, but she genuinely cares for Katie and wants to be responsible in her caring. She is fortunate that she has several resources on which to call in order both to clarify the situation and to give help. So let's continue with our conversation.

MRS. WARNER: It sounds like you've got some problems and your mom does too. Let's see if we can find some ways to help you work on yours. I'll bet your teacher, Mrs. Burnett, would have some good ideas. Let's go back to your room now, and I'll talk with her this afternoon.

KATIE        *(still a little teary):* Yes, ma'am.

MRS. WARNER  *(pulling a tissue from her pocket):* Here, Katie. You may need this. *(Pause.)* We can wait here a few minutes before we go back to your room, if you need to.

KATIE:       No, I'll be OK. *(Smiles faintly.)* Thank you, Mrs. Warner.

They walked back to the classroom, Mrs. Warner's hand on Katie's shoulder. Later that day Mrs. Warner learned from Mrs. Burnett that Katie's invalid grandmother had recently moved into their home. She was a demanding woman. Katie's mother and the rest of the family were having a very difficult time dealing with her. Katie's mother had told the school about the situation, but, until this incident, no one had realized how Katie was being affected by all that was going on at home. As a result of this sensitive encounter between Katie and Mrs. Warner, the school counselor was informed, and time was scheduled to talk with Katie about how things were going. While the situation at home could not be changed, Katie now had the opportunity to share the burden and receive support from caring people.

Let's review some of the primary ingredients that made up Mrs. Warner's caring for Katie.

1. She noticed that there appeared to be a need (awareness and beginning to gather information; chapter 2).
2. She made the decision to check it out (taking the initiative and defining herself; chapter 3).
3. She stopped and inquired about Katie's welfare (verbal and nonverbal invitation; chapter 3).
4. She listened to Katie and responded (attentive to words, feelings, and behavior; chapter 4).
5. She acknowledged her limits (self-knowledge; chapter 5).
6. She used appropriate and available resources (referral; chapter 6).

As noted earlier, care need not be confined to the crisis points in life. In fact, caring in such everyday situations provides us with greater resources for coping with more critical moments. This extended illustration of Mrs. Warner and Katie is an example of the opportunities that are constantly around us in our ordinary life. Although we have analyzed this particular incident in great detail, we hope you won't feel that caring is too much trouble if it involves this much work. Caring does require thought and energy, but thinking and responding in this way, over a period of time, will become almost automatic.

Caring is an extension of ourselves and therefore demands that we devote time and energy to developing appropriate skills. Once the discipline of caring is learned, it still requires constant fine tuning. We never really know enough. But as we grow in our caring it becomes a source of excitement rather than drudgery. When we are caught up in the joy of giving to others, we find ourselves receiving as well.

The everydayness of caring can be illustrated in many ways. The forms of caring are numerous. Here are just a few opportunities that are available every day.

1. Smiling at a stranger
2. Opening the door for someone
3. Offering to carry something for an elderly or a disabled person
4. Writing a thank-you note
5. Preparing a meal for someone during a critical time, such as illness or death
6. Reading a story to a child
7. Making a telephone call to someone who lives alone, just to see that the person is OK
8. Assisting a neighbor with home or yard maintenance
9. Offering someone a ride to church or to a shopping mall
10. Making a *genuine* inquiry about someone's welfare while waiting in line at a restaurant or a grocery store

Perhaps you thought everyday caring was more involved or more dramatic. This list could be considered simply a matter of manners. And, at one level, it is. But the way in which these extensions of care are offered makes the difference. In fact, the manner and consistency with which you present yourself in these ordinary circumstances may determine how another person responds in less ordinary times. Your seemingly insignificant and even routine invitation to someone may lead that person to turn around and invite you into his or her life in a more significant way. Your invitation is a form of the way in which God's grace comes to us. God extends grace and love to all of us, inviting but not pushing.

You may be wondering at this point, Is caring no more than just being nice? Well, it certainly starts there. After all, if you aren't "nice," who is going to ask you for help or allow you to help anyway? Being nice is a style of extending yourself to people in a regular and consistent manner—being approachable. Our intent in this book is to build on this style so that you become not only willing but able to provide care when the opportunity presents itself. Of course, along with the tools, you also need an awareness of your limits, so that you won't be overwhelmed.

There is a price in becoming involved in the life of another. We might even describe it as one of the costs of discipleship. When we choose to make ourselves available to others, we are attempting to model ourselves after Christ, who came as a servant to us. His service resulted in rejection and pain. And that is always a possibility when we enter into the pain of another. As one friend used to put it, "It is very frightening to hear someone say to you, 'I have a problem,' because if you really respond to it, then you have a problem as well." One of the values of caring within the context of a community of believers is that we can share the burden, not only with each other but with God. We will develop this concept in the next chapter.

Bear in mind also that caring is not just something for the tough times in life. It is equally important to offer our care when celebrations are in order. For example:

1. Congratulating someone on a job promotion
2. Preparing a dish to celebrate the homecoming of a new baby
3. Sending a letter of congratulations to a new graduate
4. Sharing in a wedding celebration
5. Rejoicing in the reconciliation of family members who have been alienated by conflict
6. Extending support and encouragement to a newly professing Christian
7. Welcoming a new family into the neighborhood

## Using Specific Gifts

Caring is a matter of being available—and more. It involves looking for opportunities to use the specific gifts that God has given us. When you look at it from this perspective, there are a remarkable number of ways in which caring can take place. Sarah Parker, for example, is an incredibly smart, intelligent, and productive professional woman. After her retirement, she discovered that there were a number of women over the age of sixty-five who were living on very modest pensions. Sarah's business experience had given her keen insight into the investment and management of money. So she volunteered to assist these women (and a few men as well) in wisely managing their limited assets. She didn't do the work *for* them. She taught them *how* to do it themselves. When these people fell on hard times, they often called Sarah because of the help she had given them in fiscal matters. She would listen, provide support where she could, or refer them to appropriate resources. She knew her gifts (and her limits), and she shared them in a caring way.

George Baker is another example. Was he ever an organizer! You name it, and he would organize it—systematically, efficiently, and quickly. George's church was involved in all sorts of programs: serving hot meals to the poor, providing walk-in counseling to people in an inner-city setting, organizing neighborhood groups to maintain a sense of community within the congregation.

All of this outreach was great. The trouble was that once these programs were launched, they soon collapsed. No one knew why. Great ideas came and went. So did the programs. The congregation was confused and disappointed. Then along came George! He quickly saw that programs born with great enthusiasm soon died because people were having to work far more than they had originally planned. With his organizational skills, George was able to shape ideas into programs with realistic goals and expectations. He had found his niche for caring. After listening to people voice hopes and dreams, he could translate those ideas and visions into a working reality. George's extension of himself (sharing his gifts) enabled a congregation to extend itself to others in more lasting and effective ways.

George is an example of extending self not only to individuals but to the whole community as well. The story of God's relationship to God's people, as told in scripture, is not limited to individuals. Rather, it extends to the collective group as much as it does to each member of it. Sometimes we forget that God's promises were made to the *people* of Israel, not just to Abraham. Jesus not only healed blind Bartimaeus (an individual) but was also concerned about feeding five thousand people (a group). There are many occasions when our awareness and our specific gifts can be extended to a group or a community. Some examples are:

1. A carpenter assists in building an emergency shelter for the homeless in the inner city.
2. A nurse volunteers to give physical exams to children in a day care center in a low-income area.
3. A psychologist agrees to lead a support group for divorced persons in a local parish.
4. A banker and an attorney cooperate in setting up a special trust fund to assist a new church development program.
5. An artist provides instruction in drawing for a nursing home.
6. A mechanic offers to teach automobile repair one afternoon a week to a group of teenagers.
7. A group of teenagers gives one Saturday a month to do light maintenance and repairs for disabled members of the community.

8. Put yourself here and describe what you could do for the community in which you live.

## A Brief Exercise

Opportunities for caring occur in places as simple as the line in a grocery store. Look at this situation as a case in point.

As you are standing in line, ready to check out, you run into Jim, who is ahead of you. Wishing to be polite and cordial, you say, "Hi, Jim, how are you?" Jim responds sarcastically, "Well, I'll tell you, but you may want to retract the question."

Opportunity has knocked. What do you say? We'll leave this one completely up to you. Write down some responses that seek to use the awareness and skills that we have discussed. Then evaluate them in terms of helpfulness and effectiveness.

## For Your Reflection

What more can we say? Caring is an endless expression to others of the unlimited grace that we believe has been extended to us through Jesus Christ. No one gift or skill can be discounted.

"For as in one body we have many members, and all the members do not have the same function, so we, though many, are one body in Christ, and individually members one of another" (Rom. 12:4–5).

What we hope you will do is develop the tools described in this book and use them to find ways to use your particular gifts in everyday encounters with people in your community.

*Benevolent God, we don't understand all the pain and suffering in your world, but we are grateful for your presence with us. Thank you for the day-to-day opportunities we have to share your love with each*

*other. We also offer you thanks and praise for indi-
vidual gifts that are ours to give to each other in
community. Now in your wisdom guide us to use
them not for our own selfish purposes but in ways
that will further your purposes in this world. May we
use them with the loving care that you have extended
to us in your gift of Jesus Christ. Amen.*

# 8

# Strength for Caring

At this point you may find yourself feeling overwhelmed by the number of issues that call for your attention. You may just be wondering whether you can share your caring at all! Well, the fact is that you can't—not by yourself.

In order to extend yourself with genuine caring on a regular basis, you need two essential resources: a relationship with God and a relationship with a caring community.

## Relationship with God

While the focus thus far has been on the skills of caring rather than the discipline of theology, the description of the steps of caring reflects our understanding of the ways in which God cares for us. God offers us the supreme expression of the caretaker who initiates contact with us. In chapter 3 in the section "Initiating the Relationship," three steps were described that enable our expression of such caring to begin. Consider these steps in looking at God's care for us.

### Gathering Information

There is no need for gathering to take place on the divine level, because God is the one who created us and is constantly with us. We believe that God knows our needs before we can think or ask. The Gospel of Luke tells us that none of us is forgotten, and even the hairs on our heads are numbered. "Are not five sparrows sold for two pennies? And not one of them is forgotten before God. Why, even the hairs of your head are all numbered. Fear not; you are of more value than many sparrows" (Luke 12:6–7).

## Defining Self

God is defined to us through history and through scripture as one who is faithful and just. The ultimate revelation of God's love is to be found in the life, death, and resurrection of Jesus Christ. Through that supreme act, God has been made known to us.

> And the Word became flesh and dwelt among us, full of grace and truth; we have beheld his glory, glory as of the only Son from the Father. . . . And from his fulness have we all received, grace upon grace. For the law was given through Moses; grace and truth came through Jesus Christ. No one has ever seen God; the only Son, who is in the bosom of the Father, he has made him known. (John 1:14–18)

> In many and various ways God spoke of old to our fathers by the prophets; but in these last days he has spoken to us by a Son, whom he appointed the heir of all things, through whom also he created the world. He reflects the glory of God and bears the very stamp of his nature. (Heb. 1:1–3a)

## Extending an Invitation

The gift of Jesus Christ demonstrates the lengths to which God is willing to go to extend a grace-full invitation to all of us. "For God so loved the world that he gave his only Son, that whoever believes in him should not perish but have eternal life" (John 3:16).

God constantly and consistently seeks to be in relationship with us, even when we resist. "Behold, I stand at the door and knock; if any one hears my voice and opens the door, I will come in to him and eat with him, and he with me" (Rev. 3:20).

Because we know of God's powerful love that is extended to us, we have the opportunity to claim it and be empowered by it in our caring. By doing so, we care for others in a way that both reflects God's care and makes us recipients of strength that goes far beyond what we could ever manufacture ourselves. We need to remember that what we are extending is God's care, not just our own. In fact, it is when we try to carry the entire burden of caring by ourselves that we are most prone to burn out by failing to acknowledge God's care for us and for others.

At the end of each chapter there is a brief devotional. Continue this pattern of meditation as you seek God's guidance and strength in caring for others. Effective caring begins with opening ourselves to the resources that come through God's grace and love. Some ways of doing this include prayer, reading of scripture, and gathering devotional resources. Daily connections with God are primary in our attempts to connect with others.

In chapter 4, ways of nurturing the relationship were described. Just as we are called to nurture the caring relationship with others, we are invited to open ourselves to God's nurture of us. One of the nurturing disciplines is *listening*. Listening for God's word to us is even more necessary if we are to become comfortable listening to others. As we become more assured of God's presence with us, we are better able to wait as we listen to others.

The second discipline involved in nurturing the relationship is that of *responding*. Responding involves learning more about ourselves and learning more about what is "normal" human behavior. In like fashion, as we become aware of God's reaching out to us, we are called to respond by learning more about God's grace. As our knowledge of God's presence with us increases, we are better able to communicate the assurance that God is also present with those for whom we care. It is this increased knowledge that enables us to reflect God's love more clearly and care for others more effectively.

This book cannot tell you the most helpful way for you to develop your own relationship with God, for two reasons. First, that special relationship is initiated by God. Second, you are created by God as a unique individual whose response to God's love will be reflected in ways that are authentic for you. But there is really no way that any of us can care effectively for others unless we accept God's invitation to care for us.

## Relationship with a Christian Community

When speaking of the strength that we find in God for our caring, we are describing a vertical relationship. We can also find strength and additional resources in the horizontal relationships of our faith community. We are created in the image of God, and that image is not complete apart from relationships with each other. Just as we are called to care for one another, we also need to be cared for *by* each other. To attempt to care without accepting care is, again, to rely too much on self. Such self-reliance denies the very message we are attempting to deliver—that caring is a shared ministry that we extend to each other as members of the priesthood of all believers.

In addition to the opportunities and responsibilities we share as members of this priesthood, we all possess special gifts for caring. In God's infinite wisdom, our gifts are not all alike. As the New Testament letter of 1 Corinthians puts it,

Now there are varieties of gifts, but the same Spirit; and
there are varieties of service, but the same Lord; and
there are varieties of working, but it is the same God
who inspires them all in every one. To each is given the
manifestation of the Spirit for the common good. To one
is given through the Spirit the utterance of wisdom, and
to another the utterance of knowledge according to the
same Spirit, to another faith by the same Spirit, to another gifts of healing by the one Spirit, to another the
working of miracles, to another prophecy. . . . All these
are inspired by one and the same Spirit, who apportions
to each one individually as he wills. (1 Cor. 12:4–11)

The knowledge of our different gifts and the
awareness that our needs vary leave us convinced
that all of us have special forms of caring that can and
should be expressed to others. Once we believe that
we are called to care for each other, then we have the
responsibility to become aware of and then develop
our particular gifts for caring.

## A Charge

This book has focused primarily on you as an individual caregiver. But do not think that you must (or
can) carry this burden alone. You need the vertical
strength of God's grace and the horizontal resources
of a community of faith to give you support. One of
the best ways to use these resources is through an
organized caring group within a congregation. Some
churches call them shepherding programs; others
call them pastoral care groups. Whatever the name,
the aim is the same—sharing the opportunities and
responsibilities of caring while using each individual's gifts.

Our prayer for you is that you will experience the
richness of God's care in your own life in a way that
frees you to reach out to others. That, in the final

analysis, is the power that enables us to share our caring with each other.

*Now may the God of peace who brought again from the dead our Lord Jesus, the great shepherd of the sheep, by the blood of the eternal covenant, equip you with everything good that you may do his will, working in you that which is pleasing in his sight, through Jesus Christ; to whom be glory for ever and ever. Amen. (Heb. 13:20–21)*

# Appendix
## Using This Book in Caring Groups

One of the most valuable personal resources for your caring can come from a group. Some churches organize shepherding or pastoral committees in which the members share the caring responsibilities within the parish. In other congregations, elected officers often carry out these duties along with the pastor. We are called to care as individuals, but as you have seen from this book, caring often can be more effective when shared.

If you are not presently involved in a caring group within your congregation or community, you may want to look around to see what is already available. If you find that there is no caring group that you can join, you could consider starting one.

Invite a few friends into your home from your church, neighborhood, or place of business. Share some ideas about how you as a group can be more intentional and effective in your caring. You might suggest that they read this book as background for your conversations. The exercises that are provided at the end of many of the chapters could be used to test each other's skills.

After a period of familiarization (such as six to eight weekly sessions) with these basic concepts and skills, you might move to some kind of organized system for alerting the group about people in need. A method for regular hospital visitation could be developed. Even more important, develop a plan for keeping in touch with persons who have returned home from the hospital or who are recovering from an illness. Whatever you set up, keep it simple. Don't become so organized that it becomes burdensome. Remember that we are interested in sharing our caring, not inflicting it on anyone.

If you are a church officer and want to develop a caring group within your congregation, discuss it with your pastor and plan a shepherding group together. You may want to plan a special retreat to introduce the idea to other officers or to the larger congregation. Material and exercises from this book can be used to guide interested persons into effective skills in Christian caring. Special leadership for the occasion may draw even more attention to the importance of caring in the church's life.

From this base, you can then develop your own organizational structure that suits the specific caring needs of your congregation. Again, make things simple so that people will want to be involved. Stress the importance of sharing the caring so that no one person carries the burden alone.

# Further Reading

Described below are a few of the books that could serve as helpful additional resources to you in your ongoing development of caring groups. The literature in the field generally refers to this sort of caring as "lay ministry."

Detwiler-Zapp, Diane, and William C. Dixon. *Lay Caregiving.* Philadelphia: Fortress Press, 1982.
A psychotherapist and a Presbyterian minister combined their professional skills to develop a program of caring in a local congregation. This book describes their rationale and specific guidelines for their work.

Hahn, Celia A., James R. Adams, and Anne G. Amy. *My Struggle to Be a Caring Person.* Support for Laity in Their Ministries, Vol. 1. Washington, D.C.: Alban Institute, 1981.
This book describes systematic programs of care developed in several parishes at the same time. Anyone in need of an outline for a series of training sessions on caring will find this book a helpful resource.

Southard, Samuel. *Comprehensive Pastoral Care: Enabling the Laity to Share in Pastoral Ministry.* Valley Forge, Pa.: Judson Press, 1975.
Professor Southard directs his discussion to or-

dained clergy, but don't think that you are eliminated if you aren't ordained. You can benefit from his helpful descriptions of the nature of caring. He effectively sensitizes us to human need and provides practical guidelines for strengthening caring resources in a community. In 1982 he developed his thought further in *Training Church Members for Pastoral Care*, again with Judson Press.

Stone, Howard W. *The Caring Church: A Guide for Lay Pastoral Care.* San Francisco: Harper & Row, 1983.

Professor Stone combines brief, helpful discussions of the nature of caring with practical, step-by-step guidelines for the training of church members for the ministry of caring in a local congregation.

Wright, Frank. *Pastoral Care for Lay People*. London: SCM Press, 1982.

Canon Wright wrote this book to encourage your thinking about pastoral care and its importance in congregational life. Though he provides no practical guidelines on the establishment of a program, his thoughts about the nature and importance of caring are quite helpful.